CW01661880

HOW TO STOP BEING TOXIC?

Break Free from Narcissistic Behaviors and Negative Thinking to Build Unbreakable Relationships and Achieve Inner Peace

By

Emily Harper

Kindle ISBN: 978-1-917358-14-9

Paperback ISBN: 978-1-917358-15-6

Hardcover ISBN: 978-1-917358-16-3

Contents

Introduction: The Path Towards

A profound loneliness washed over him as Alan brushed his fingers across his awards. Today was supposed to be the most important day of his life; he had just won the "Best Actor Male" award for his blockbuster movie. Millions of fans adored Alan, yet there was no one beside him. He stared at the prize he held tightly, his eyes froze at his reflection. The voice of his long-lost love echoed in his mind, "I will always remain by your side."

He closed his eyes tightly, trying to control his emotions. He remembered the hurtful words of his best friend Ross, "You have become a big man with a little heart." Alan could hardly fathom how much he had hurt Ross. As he gazed at his reflection, he glimpsed the wreckage of his narcissism. Tears formed in Alan's eyes as he stumbled to his feet, feeling as lonely as a person. He had never imagined that the consequences of his selfish and narcissistic actions would be so overwhelming. There was a void in his soul that could only be filled by the loved ones he had pushed away.

The next day, Alan called Ross and apologized. He was sincere in his intentions. He also called his long-lost love and tried to make up to her. Alan remembered that he had always treated her girlfriend unfairly and blamed her for every conflict. He also went to his parents and asked for forgiveness. He had not been in contact with them for almost two years. Alan was devoted to becoming a better person and breaking free from narcissism. He knew the journey ahead would be long and arduous, but with his loved ones by his side, he believed it would be worth it.

Years passed, and Alan remained determined in his transformation. His relationships blossomed, and he finally understood the true meaning of success and satisfaction. No longer did he crave the love of many; the love of his cherished ones was all he needed. Alan had found fulfillment, not in the masses' adoration, but in the genuine connections he had rebuilt.

You must be proud of Alan for having the courage to walk the path of betterment. But remember, by turning to this first page of the book, you also show your bravery in taking the first step toward becoming the best version of yourself. So, I am proud of you for not remaining in the same negative mindset and for striving to improve.

Purpose of this Book

There are many times when you may have unintentionally hurt your loved ones. You say mean and awful things, and later, you deeply regret them. You strive to keep those around you happy but often fail despite your best efforts. Sometimes, in your craving for attention and praise, you belittle others. Do you feel like a wall has been built between you and your loved ones? Have you ever wondered if your actions or theirs created this wall? There would have been many moments when you realized your mistake and wanted to change. Imagine if you knew the art of handling conflicts with care and sincerity. You would respect other people's boundaries and understand their point of view. Your relationships begin to flourish, and everyone around you is happy to be with you.

You become healthier and happier, no longer manipulating others or craving validation. This book will guide you toward that transformation. I assure you that soon, you will break free from negative thinking and toxic traits. Happiness and love will start chasing you, leading to healthy, long-lasting relationships. You will experience the true meanings of confidence, trust, and hope. You'll discover profound peace from harmony with your mind and yourself. Take a deep breath and turn the page if you are ready to start the most beautiful journey of healing and self-growth.

Section 1: Discovering Yourself, Unlocking True Wealth

Chapter 1: Unveiling the Monsters Within

We all have dark shadows within us that we sometimes fail to fight. These fears, insecurities and negative patterns shape our behaviors. This chapter will unveil the monsters holding you back from living your best life. You tend to ignore your insecurities and thus develop defensive ways to hide them. It would help if you remembered that every soul has a unique purpose. You need to learn specific lessons to bring a positive change in your personality. You will learn about your flaws and insecurities but with the mindset of growth.

Decoding Toxicity

It is hard to admit that you have toxic behaviors when you have developed them for a long time. In this section, we will start to uncover what toxicity means. It is essential to spot toxic behaviors so that you can get rid of them as soon as possible. When you become aware of the toxicity, you develop the strength to step away from it and follow the path of positivity.

What is Toxicity?

Toxicity refers to acting in ways that cause conflict, harm, and unpleasantness in the lives of those around you. It encompasses actions and behaviors that gradually harm others and create a toxic environment. Like a termite, toxicity slowly erodes the love and trust in your relationships. Eventually, all that remains are arguments, fights, and accusations.

But why do you fail to kill this termite and instead kill your relationships?

You may think that being a toxic person is easy. You just need to manipulate people, never admitting your mistakes or being selfish. But if you look closely, you will see all the insecurities, overthinking and trauma toxic people have been going through all the years of their lives. They also carry this emotional baggage to their workplace, college, hangouts with friends and even at home. To hide this emotional baggage, toxic people tend to show dominance and criticize other people.

To better understand toxicity, let's read the story of Anna and Ember below.

Two sisters, Anna and Ember, lovingly tended to a beautiful garden. This garden, a cherished gift from their parents, was filled with elegant white lilies and vibrant red roses. The sound of birds and the fresh morning breeze welcomed the villagers, making it a beloved spot for everyone.

The sisters were sincere about their garden and thus watered it daily and took care of the plants. However, one day, Anna felt something strange. The flowers on the side of Ember's garden started turning yellow. It seemed as if they had lost their beauty. The soil around them also became dry, withering the plants. Anna became extremely worried and went to discuss the matter with Ember.

"Ember, your flowers are withering, and it seems nobody is taking care of them," Anna said with concern.

"What do you mean I don't take good care of them? It's not me, it's the weather! The weather is so harsh that the seeds do not grow. Next time, I will buy good quality seeds myself." Ember replied defensively.

Anna was aware that seeds and the weather were not in any way wrong. Ember was just not ready to take responsibility, so Anna decided to investigate this situation herself.

Anna started noticing Ember's actions and soon discovered she had been using solid fertilizer to grow her plants faster. However, Ember was unaware of the consequences and not concerned about them. She just wanted her part of the garden to be the best.

Anna confronted Ember about her actions and warned her that all her flowers would soon die, and no one would come to her part of the garden if she didn't stop. Now extremely worried, Ember began searching for solutions to the damage she had caused. Anna made Ember realize that it was never about whose part of the garden was better but about caring for the garden together, just as their parents had wished.

Anna helped Ember remove the toxic soil and plant new seeds in the fresh and healthy soil. Together, they watered the plants daily, and soon, Ember's part of the garden was once again filled with beautiful and fresh flowers. These flowers stood as a testament that competition with one another brings harm, but working together and helping each other brings positive outcomes for everyone.

You need to realize that toxic behavior, like artificial fertilizer, can eventually erode and harm your relationships, even if its intention is good. It's time to understand these poisonous behaviors and eliminate them for the sake of healthier and happier relationships.

Importance of Awareness of Toxic Behavior

It's essential to be well aware of toxic behaviors. The main problem with toxicity is that it can be present in you and your loved ones too, but you don't want to believe it. You often overlook harmful patterns if they are present in you. However, it is essential to notice these toxic behaviors for your mental well-being.

To observe toxic behaviors, you need to start observing your actions more closely. Do you react positively when someone tells you that you hurt them? Do you listen to others' concerns with heart, or do you become defensive and give excuses? Do you celebrate your achievements or degrade others to make them feel small?

These observations are crucial because actions prove more than words. If you constantly tell someone that you love them but always disrespect them, then it means that you are lying. Love is not something to be expressed through words but rather actions.

Observing these behaviors, even in your close ones, is essential to protect your emotional well-being.

Being aware of toxicity in yourself is the first step in protecting yourself from negativity. Toxic people often hide their insecurities by judging and insulting other people. If you are one of them, you will drain energy, hurt, and make others emotionally weak. You must guard your positive energy and avoid negative influences that could diminish your positivity.

Recognizing Toxic Reactions to Your Success

You also need to recognize that the success of others can trigger toxic reactions. When faced with someone else's achievements, you might feel a surge of insecurity that leads to disrespecting or undermining them. These behaviors often stem from your own unresolved insecurities.

For instance, if a person is trying to lose weight and look good, a toxic person might start accusing them of gaining attention from other people.

This is because they take others as a competition and become insecure.

Similarly, if your friend got a promotion, you might want him to humble himself. You might start to highlight his flaws and thus make him feel small. This is a significant indication of jealousy and being insecure about him.

Your reactions can reveal a lot about the feelings you have for others.

Self-Reflection for Those Who Might Be Toxic

You might recognize that these toxic traits are present in you. It will help if you start questioning your insecurities that force you to act poisonously. Understanding your insecurities can allow you to change your behavior and resolve the underlying issues. Overcoming your insecurities can make your relationship healthier and allow you to live a happier life. Being aware of your toxic traits can help you overcome them, leading to a more favorable environment for everyone around you.

Common Traits and Behaviors

Now, we have understood what it means to be toxic and how crucial it is to be aware of it. *Following are some common traits that can be seen in a toxic person.*

- ***This Person is Extremely Unfamiliar.***

The most common trait about a toxic person is that they do not seem familiar. You feel you don't know them, no matter how close you both are. They never reveal their true identities and intentions. Toxic people are afraid that telling too much about themselves will expose their fears and insecurities. They never share their personal details even with their close ones.

If you want to recognize such toxic traits, you should pay attention to how you speak about yourself.

Do you speak consciously so that nobody judges you? Do you make up stories, or do you tell genuine experiences? A toxic person would always try to make up stories and lie to hide their insecurities.

- ***They Always Want to Focus on Themselves.***

A toxic person often wants to be the center of attention. This is because they have so much built-up trauma that when things don't go their way, their anxiety starts to build. They worry that something terrible will happen, similar to past experiences. As a result, they try to control the situation and act selfishly, even if it hurts others.

It's important to recognize these patterns in yourself and others. If you feel insecure when someone else scores higher than you or if you get upset when a coworker receives a bonus, it's a sign that you need to change these habits. Holding onto these toxic behaviors will ultimately harm your relationships and your well-being.

- ***They Always Want to be Admired.***

A toxic person always wants to be in the good books of others. This often means that they will blame someone else without a second thought. If someone questions their reputation, they become highly defensive. They hurt and disrespect the other person just to maintain their image in front of others.

- ***They Show No Effort.***

A toxic person will never try to make efforts for the other person. They are so self-centered that they never care for the other person's feelings. Even if they do something nice for their loved ones, they constantly remind them of their efforts. They manipulate others into thinking that they are the best for them and that others should never leave them. It is essential to understand such people's behavior to protect yourself from their manipulation.

Different Types of Toxic Personalities

The people you hang out with have the most power over you. If they have bad energy, they will most likely destroy your life. You need to choose your friends rather than make them. Be friends with people with a positive aura who want the best for you. Here are the major types of toxic people that would negatively influence your life.

1. Thief

These types of toxic people pretend to be your friends but are secretly jealous of you. They want the same good things that happen to you to happen to them. Their level of toxicity is so high that they will start to copy you or even sabotage your entire life. Being aware of such friends is crucial because they are not easily recognized. They may seem supportive and appreciative, but deep down, they envy your achievements. Recognizing this hidden jealousy can help protect you from their harmful intentions.

2. Snake

These are the types of toxic people who love to gossip and say bad things about others. They act like true friends to your face but talk badly about you behind your back. Being extremely judgmental, they focus too much on others, criticizing what people wear or who they are friends with. They will listen to all your rants and then spread them to everyone. Being aware of such people is crucial, as their behavior can harm and damage your reputation.

3. Energy Takers

These people always play the victim and drain everyone's energy around them. They thrive on drama and stir up conflicts even at the slightest inconvenience. Being around them often creates a negative aura and leaves others feeling exhausted. Recognizing these traits is essential, as it helps protect your well-being and maintain healthy relationships.

4. Controllers

These are the types of toxic people who always want to dominate others and control everyone's life around them. They do this because they believe that they were not given much control in their childhood. As a result, this insecurity is built up inside them, which makes them act this way.

5. The Takers

These are toxic people who always ask for favors and do not respect your boundaries. They do not care about your time and money and would just think about themselves. They would never reciprocate the same efforts as you do and would make you feel like a bad guy if you ever said "NO" to their needs.

6. The Bad influence

These people vibrate at a low energy level and always try to pull you down. They would intentionally give you advice, which would have dire consequences in the future. The advice may include leaving your final assignment at the last minute to enjoy a party or resigning from a job to live a stress-free life.

Effects of Toxic Behaviors

According to the American entrepreneur and author, Jim Rohn, a person is always the average of five people he spends most of his time with. This means you are a combination of the people you mostly hang out with. Friendships have the most influence on you. If you have toxic friends, you will soon start behaving like them. Your mindset and habits will begin to change in a poisonous way. If you want a successful life, you should have a friend circle with a positive mindset and goals.

Time for Self-Check

Sit back and close your eyes. I want you to remember each of your friends and write down their names on paper. Once you have written down their names, separately observe their impact on you and your life.

Here are a few questions that might help you in this activity:

1. *What are my feelings after I hang out with this friend?*
2. *Do we have any shared goals that we want to accomplish?*
3. *Does he/she put effort into our friendship?*
4. *What are the five things that I admire about our friendship?*
5. *Does he/she guide me towards the right or the wrong?*

Stories from the Shadows

Understanding human behaviors is quite tricky as everybody is different and has unique life experiences. Thus, it becomes hard for psychologists to develop theories regarding human behaviors. This section will explore the works of psychologists who have helped us understand the underlying issues behind our reactions. Imagine that you are walking through a dense forest, and the shadows are lurking over you. You are afraid and uncertain of the things that lie ahead.

This part of the book is like a light that will guide you through the forest and help you explore exciting theories told by many psychologists. You will also meet unforgettable characters who will tell you all about their stories! As you walk through this part, you will understand the reactions, emotions and insecurities behind a toxic response.

Psychological Theories

Psychology has always unfolded the human mind. Many psychologists have come together to discover astounding theories that define how we act. Let's have a look at them!

1. Theory of Projection by Freud

Sigmund Freud had a keen interest in human behaviors and personalities. One day, he noticed a man named Klaus who had extreme jealousy issues. He used to accuse his wife of infidelity, although she was loyal to him. Freud started experimenting with Klaus and carried out many sessions with him. Throughout these sessions, Freud realized that Klaus had a fantasy of cheating on his partner and suppressed his desires. As a result, he used to express his guilt by projecting his insecurities on his wife. This experiment discovered that people who behave in a toxic manner often blame others to avoid damaging their own image.

2. Social Learning Theory by Albert Bandura

Albert Bandura was a Swiss psychologist interested in learning about people's behaviors. He carried out an experiment in which he noticed that people understand behaviors based on observations. To confirm this, he carried out an experiment in which children were taken as the control group. These children used to imitate the toxic behaviors of adults towards a doll. It showed that these children used to copy their adults and behave exactly as their adults. It proved that the children who grow up in a toxic environment also do toxic actions in their relationships.

3. Dominance Theory by Karen Horney

Karen Horney believed that individuals who showed dominance have deep-rooted insecurities. He carried out an experiment in which he observed a man named George. George used to show power and control over other people. Karen followed him for a few days and concluded that his toxic behavior of manipulating and unnecessarily dominating others was due to defending himself in situations that would lead to helplessness.

4. Development Theory by Erik Erikson

Erik, a successful psychologist, once had a case involving a patient. His patient was incredibly selfish and used to manipulate people for his benefit. Erik observed him keenly and learnt that human behavior has eight developmental stages:

1. Trust vs. Mistrust: Infancy, 0-1 years
2. Autonomy vs. Shame and Doubt: Early Childhood, 1-3 years
3. Initiative vs. Guilt: Preschool, 3-6 years
4. Industry vs. Inferiority: School Age, 6-12 years
5. Identity vs. Role Confusion: Adolescence, 12-18 years
6. Intimacy vs. Isolation: Young Adulthood, 18-40 years
7. Generativity vs. Stagnation: Middle Adulthood, 40-65 years
8. Integrity vs. Despair: Late Adulthood, 65+ years

The patient struggled in the "Identity vs. Role" stage when he was an adolescent. As a result, he manipulated others to atone for his unresolved identity.

Real-Life Researches

• Digital Narcissism

Research on "Digital Narcissism" was carried out by Tomas Chamorro-Premuzic in 2023 to learn about the toxic behaviors influenced by social media. The main focus of this research was the impact that the number of likes and comments had on people who used excessive social media. A more profound observation in this research concluded that people developed less self-confidence and started seeking validation from others. They compared themselves with models and influencers on Instagram, which created feelings of jealousy and inadequacy. These feelings can lead to back-biting, spreading rumors and hurting others.

Self-Check Assessment

- *Have you ever found yourself constantly checking for likes and comments for a recent post?*
- *Have you ever felt envious when you see your friend's story of them enjoying their life?*

If yes, then do not worry. These feelings are common in today's generation, but remember that it is essential to keep them in moderation.

- **Survival of the Fittest**

As an adult, being under economic pressure is unhealthy and can lead to a hyper-competitive environment. Research conducted by Rohitha Naraharisetty in 2021, in a few offices showed that coworkers sabotage, take undue credit, and even spread rumors to get a higher position in the job sector. This economic uncertainty and pressure act as a breeding ground for toxic behaviors.

Self-Check Assessment

- *What are your thoughts regarding team success?*
- *Have you ever felt job insecurity?*
- *Do you think you have constant competition with your coworkers?*

If yes, I can help you shift your mindset towards a more positive one.

- **Helicopter Parenting**

A study on "Helicopter Parenting" was carried out by Dr. Jennifer and Dr. David in 2018. This study showed that individuals who were brought up by controlling parents were more dependent on others. They also showed higher levels of manipulative personalities. For instance, a girl named Sarah was brought up by over-controlling parents. She couldn't handle rejection well and went into depression. She also tried to manipulate her colleagues and turn situations in her favor. This study has proved that parents play a vital role in a child's upbringing and personality development.

Self-Check Assessment

- *How do you feel about your parents? Do you have any issues with them?*
- *Like Sarah, have you ever faced rejection as an insult?*
- *Have you ever tried to manipulate others and not care about their feelings?*

The Drama and Conflict Lovers

Another research by Dr. Laura and Dr. Michael in 2o20 showed the impact of social media on people and their behaviors. It proved that people start behaving like their favorite characters from a movie or drama. For instance, if a person watches a film in which their favorite character lies or manipulates others, they will likely start behaving like the character and apply similar manipulation tricks in their real lives. The behavior shown by celebrities in movies or dramas has a very powerful impact on society. People adopt the way these celebrities behave and get themselves into conflicts and dramas, which has a very negative impact on their lives and relationships.

Self-Check Assessment:

- *Do you find yourself constantly thinking of a movie character and their behaviors?*
- *Do you try to act in the same way your favorite celebrity does?*
- *Do you try to resolve conflicts the way the characters from a drama do?*

Real-Life Stories

From Shadows to Spotlight: Paul's Journey to Genuine Success

Paul had always been a guy who thrived on being the center of attention. At work, he would often take credit for things his coworkers did, soaking up all the praise. But as time passed, his need to be admired grew more intense. He started doing whatever it took to stay in the spotlight, even if it meant deceiving his friends. Slowly, people began to drift away from him, and Paul felt more and more alone.

One day, Paul attended a corporate seminar, not expecting much to come of it. But then he heard the speaker, Sarah, a successful businesswoman who talked about teamwork and the importance of genuine relationships. She said something that stuck with him: **"A candle loses nothing when it lights another candle."** *Those words hit Paul hard. They made him think about how he had been living his life.*

He realized that his actions were driven by fear of being overshadowed and losing his job if someone else got ahead. These fears stemmed from old insecurities and past traumas he had never dealt with. Paul knew he needed to change.

So, he started making small changes. Instead of taking credit, he began congratulating his colleagues on their achievements. He got involved in team projects and focused on being supportive rather than competitive. Over time, Paul noticed a shift. People started trusting him again, and he felt a new happiness—a genuine sense of fulfillment from being part of a team.

After a few months, Paul had utterly transformed. His relationships were more potent, and he felt at peace with himself and those around him. He learned that he could become a better person by letting go of his fears and insecurities. Paul's story shows that you can turn your life around and find true happiness with effort and the desire to change.

From Blame Game to Love

Ruther was the guy everyone loved having around. He had this natural charm, a great sense of humor, and always seemed to have it all together. But there was one big problem—he could never admit when he was wrong. No matter what went down, Ruther found a way to pin the blame on someone else. His need to always look perfect meant he never took responsibility for his mistakes, and that started to take a toll on his relationships.

Emma, his girlfriend, really tried to make it work. She dealt with the constant arguments, hoping Ruther would eventually see things her way. She just wanted him to admit that they both had issues to work on. But Ruther's stubbornness made it impossible. He refused to see his part in their problems, and it only pushed Emma further away. Finally, she reached her breaking point and decided to end things.

Ruther felt Emma's absence deeply, but his pride kept him from reaching out. To him, acknowledging that he missed her—or, even worse, admitting he was wrong—felt like a sign of weakness. So, he remained silent, despite the emptiness her absence had created in his life.

A few weeks later, Ruther went to a friend's wedding. Watching the couple exchange vows, their love and respect for each other so evident, it hit Ruther like a ton of bricks. He realized what he had lost. After the ceremony, he ended up having a deep conversation with his friend, who didn't hold back. His friend helped him see that avoiding responsibility was a major issue in all his relationships.

That conversation shook Ruther to his core. He knew he had to change if he ever wanted to fix his relationships and find real happiness. So, he took a long, hard look at himself and started making things right. He reached out to the people he had hurt, sincerely apologized, and owned up to his mistakes.

When Ruther called Emma, it wasn't just to say he was sorry. He opened up about his flaws and told her how much he regretted the way he had treated her. His honesty struck a chord with Emma, and they decided to give their relationship another shot.

As Ruther worked on being more accountable and sincere, he saw changes all around him. His friends, his coworkers, even his parents—everyone started to see him differently. Ruther realized that real happiness didn't come from pretending to be perfect. It came from facing his flaws, owning up to them, and putting in the work to become a better person. He learned that true strength is about never making mistakes; it's about taking responsibility and doing the hard work to improve.

Spotting The Toxicity Within

Sometimes, we are so surrounded by our toxicity that we fail to see it. We overlook the poisonous ways we behave because we have become blind to our actions. We judge people continuously but need to judge where we are wrong. The following part of the book is not about judging you; rather, it is about shining a light onto your soul and seeing the toxic behaviors hidden by the darkness. It will allow you to learn about yourself and heal yourself in a fun and creative way. These worksheets and exercises are designed so that you will start to explore your inner self!

Let's get started!

Worksheet 1: Toxic Trait Mind Map

This worksheet will help you to explore your toxic traits so that you can get rid of them!

Instructions:

1. Draw a circle and write "My Toxic Traits" in the center of it.
2. Now from the center of the circle, extend branches and write different areas of your life. They may include; work, social life, and personal life.
3. Now, take a few moments to analyze yourself and recognize the toxic behaviors in yourself and how they impact each area of your life.
4. Write them down under the branches and beside each of the toxic behavior, try to pen down the reason you do this.

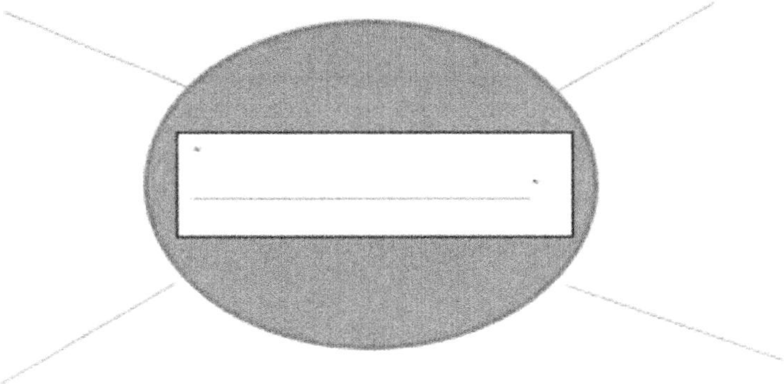

Worksheet 2: Toxic Trait Bingo

This worksheet will allow you to identify the toxic traits that you have and also those around you.

Instructions:

Mark each square as you notice yourself engaging in that behavior. Take time to reflect on the triggers and consequences of these behaviors after each row is completed and note them in your journal.

Aggression	Stealing attention	Holding Grudges	Criticizing others
Running away from responsibility	Being overly critical	A constant need for dominance	Blaming others
Seeking Attention	Treating someone with silence	Acting Defensive	Competing with someone
Manipulation	Being self-centered	Infidelity	Inflexibility

Chapter 2:
A Trip to the Narcissistic Maze

Imagine trying to find your way through a maze, where every turn brings you face-to-face with reflections that distort reality. A narcissistic person feels the same way. It can be confusing and overwhelming for a narcissistic person to deal with his own toxic behaviors. In this chapter, we will walk through this maze together. We will explore narcissism and its complexities together and try to help you overcome them. This chapter will help you find your true self and pave the way for developing better personality traits!

Unmasking Narcissism

Narcissism can be hard to understand. This is because there are many underlying issues related to narcissism that cannot be seen easily. A narcissistic person may be self-confident and self-centered. However, they only pretend to be such by masking their insecurities. In this chapter, we will understand what really lies behind that mask. Whether narcissism is about yourself or someone else, this chapter will help you to get a deeper understanding of it.

Narcissism as a Disorder

Do you have anyone in life who thinks that they are the perfect human being and are better than everyone else around them? They cannot handle the bare minimum of criticism and start a conflict.

Narcissism is a term that is now widely used in our generation. However, people are unaware of what it means. Narcissism is a personality disorder in which the human brain tricks the person into feeling that they have an unjustifiably high sense of importance.

A Greek river god, Cephisuss, had a son named Narcissus. He was charming with exceptional beauty. Everyone adored his attractive features and loved him. As he grew older, his looks became more striking, and people fell more in love with him. However, Narcissus never cared about anyone else and mistreated them. He was handsome on the outside but cruel on the inside.

One day, a beautiful young lady named Echo fell in love with Narcissus. When she expressed her love to him, he rejected her harshly and asked her never to show her face again. Echo was heartbroken and decided to leave the forest. The only thing she left behind was her voice, which could be heard all over the forest.

The goddess Nemesis witnessed everything and thought of teaching Narcissus a lesson. It was time that Narcissus paid for his insensitive actions and words. She guided Narcissus to a clear and still pool of water. As soon as Narcissus bent down to drink water from the pool, he saw his reflection and was stunned. He observed his alluring features and loved his reflection in the water.

He was so much in love that he spent many days and nights staring at his reflection. He never left the pool and didn't eat or sleep as he was so obsessed with himself.

Soon, Narcissus realized that it was his image and he could never touch or kiss it. He discovered the heart-wrenching truth that his love would never be acknowledged and returned.

This truth left him so devastated that he took his own life. After his death, the Gods turned him into a flower as a lesson for everyone. This flower, Narcissus, only grows near the water and teaches us the importance of compassion and care for others' feelings. This story shows us that if we get too self-centered and selfish, it could lead to harmful impacts on everyone's life, including us.

Narcissism is often tossed around by people with them, not realizing that this is a psychological disorder and has the same importance as the other disorders. People suffering from Narcissistic Personality Disorder (NPD) have a boosted idea of themselves and always crave attention. They are very much in love with the image of themselves that they have created in their minds. However, they fail to realize this is only due to low self-confidence and self-esteem.

Narcissism vs. Narcissistic Personality Disorder

People often confuse someone who is self-absorbed as having a narcissistic personality disorder. We need to realize that narcissism and NPD are two different things. Psychologists refer to narcissism as a trait. On the other hand, NPD is mental instability and is an illness that needs to be treated soon. It poses adverse effects on the person suffering from NPD and those around him. It's not necessary that if you have narcissistic traits, then you must fit in the criteria for NDP.

Why Understanding Narcissism Matters

You might think that being a narcissist is fun. You can have all the attention and betray others without considering their feelings. But let me tell you something. Narcissism is no fun game. A person suffering from narcissism has so much trauma and insecurities built up inside them that they create a fake wall of a sense of high self to hide it. You may not realize it, but a selfish person might be your favorite celebrity, boss, co-worker, neighbor, friend, or even partner.

Do you have a friend who stays up late to talk to you about himself? He tells you all about his new car and job. But as soon as you tell him about your achievements, he hangs up the phone.

Narcissists tend to hide their feelings of inadequacy. They get satisfied when they become the center of attention. They do not care about other people's feelings and always dominate a conversation. Here are a few reasons behind this dominance of narcissists:

- ***A Need for Approval:*** Narcissists always desire to get appraised and thus talk about their achievements. They get satisfied when a person is impressed by them.
- ***High Levels of Self-importance:*** Narcissists always think that they are better than others and their opinions hold more value. They do not care about your views and feelings because they never

respected you in the first place. Even if you propose a great idea, a narcissist would always make it sound like it is absurd.

- ***Masking their Insecurities:*** Narcissists have deep-rooted insecurities that they want to hide from the world. As a defense mechanism, they speak too much about themselves so that others would be impressed by them.
- ***Absence of Empathy:*** Narcissists have no empathy for other people's feelings and often dominate the conversations. They do not have enough ability or mental level to understand the feelings of others.

SELF-ANALYSIS QUESTIONS:

Has anyone ever told you that you're arrogant or need to humble yourself? Have you ever been in those situations where you felt over the moon when you knew you were the center of attention? Do people often call you cocky or self-centered? Narcissistic personality disorder forces a person to think arrogantly and have no respect for other's feelings and boundaries.

Red Flags and Indicators

A person suffering from NPD is stuck in a pattern of selfish and arrogant thinking. The ones close to them often call them self-obsessed, manipulative, demanding, and pretentious. They behave in toxic ways in every area of their life, whether personal or professional.

Here are a few toxic signs and symptoms that you can use to identify if you or any person you know has NDP.

1. Exaggerated Feelings of Self-Importance

Narcissists believe that they belong to a "unique" group of people, and only the members of those groups can understand how they behave. They think that they have unrealistic superiority over other people and are too remarkable to be considered average. They relate themselves to people belonging to the higher and upper classes.

Narcissists always expect to be complimented and recognized. They often over-emphasize their achievements and their positive traits. Once you get into a conversation with them, all you will hear are their efforts to make their loved ones happy, their intellect that got them a good job, or how blessed people are to have them.

2. Feelings of Privilege

As explained above, narcissists think of themselves as special people and thus want to be treated specially. They expect you to give them everything they desire. They feel that they are valuable enough to get whatever they want. However, if you ask them to reciprocate the same efforts, they will get extremely aggressive and start a conflict.

3. Constant Demand for Appraisal

A narcissist's ego is like a balloon that needs admiration to be inflated in the air. They demand constant pampering and compliments to feed their egos. They only interact with people for their use and make friends with those who can cater to their demands. These connections are incredibly one-sided. It's never about the narcissist helping the admirer; it's always about the other way around. Furthermore, the narcissist views any disruption or decline in the admirer's focus and appreciation as a betrayal.

4. Living in Their Own World

Narcissists have a world, where everyone admires them. They have unrealistic expectations of success, power, and intelligence. They feel like they are the most attractive person in the room and nobody compares to them. They try to control everyone around them and act defensively if anyone tries to pop up their bubble of imaginary world. Narcissists create such fantasies to avoid feelings and thoughts of inadequacy.

5. Belittling and Shaming Others

If narcissists meet someone from whom they feel insecure, they start to insult that person. They cannot bear it if someone appears more confident, attractive, or intellectual than them. They would do anything to put the image of that person down, whether they have to deceive them or lie about them. Narcissists also view people as objects that they can use. As a result, they think that people have no feelings and humiliate them if things don't go their way.

6. Ego and the Desire for Achievement

If we look closely, narcissism has a strong connection with self-esteem. Throughout their development, children go through various stages where they develop self-esteem. This is essential because it helps them overcome difficulties and challenges. This development of self-esteem is affected by interaction with friends and family.

Psychology has unfolded that narcissism mainly stems from the negligence of the emotional needs in the developing stages of a child. Many parents view their children as objects through which they can portray an image of good parents. They only tend to show the positive sides of their children and glorify them in front of others. They set up fictitious expectations in their child's minds and force them to be perfect. As a result, these children grow up constantly wanting to be perfect and loved by all. They want people to respect and admire them based on their beauty and intellect. They create a false self that needs validation from others, or it will collapse.

It's not necessary that narcissism only occurs through parent's negligence, but many other factors can cause it. Suppose a person is treated with criticism regularly. In that case, they might develop a false reputation that they would need to maintain to gain respect.

Just as Narcissus was tricked into falling in love with himself, narcissists are also tricked from the beginning to be perfect to get love.

Narcissists hide feelings that might bring shame and portray them as weak. Suppressing their real feelings leaves a fragile and immature person that requires constant validation.

Mirror, Mirror: Types of Narcissists

Imagine stepping into a room filled with mirrors, each showing a different version of the person in front of you. Some mirrors reveal a confident, almost larger-than-life figure, while others show someone more hidden, quieter, but self-focused in their way. That's what it's like when trying to understand the different faces of narcissism. Each type of narcissist is like a different reflection—some loud and attention-grabbing, others subtle but still self-centered. In this section, we'll look at these varied reflections. By understanding the various types of narcissists, we can start to make sense of the confusing, often contradictory behaviors we encounter and learn how to handle them more effectively. Let's look into these mirrors and uncover the real story behind the reflections.

Types of Narcissists

Below are the most common types of narcissists. You can read all scenarios and see how different types of narcissists react in different situations. You can identify and relate your behavior with these situations to know about your type and how you can behave like a normal person to avoid being a narcissist.

- **Bully Narcissists**

These are the types of narcissists that are very unfair and exhibit great power and control over other people. They try to control their lives, and if the other person shows resentment, they humiliate and degrade them. When these narcissists make other people look inferior, this gives them a self-boost and their ego gets satisfied. The primary sign of such narcissists is that they are highly aggressive and rude.

Here's an activity that will help you identify a bully narcissist and determine if you might be one yourself.

A scenario is given below. Think of your reaction, and compare it with the average person's reaction and the reaction of a bully narcissist. You've got to be really honest here.

Evaluate your response and determine what it most closely resembles.

Scenario

A team meeting is happening, and different people are expressing their views.

Normal Person's Reaction:

A normal person would try to listen to and respect everyone's points of view. They would also accept constructive criticism and maintain a positive environment.

Bully Narcissist's Reaction

A bully narcissist would continue to dismiss other people's ideas and opinions. If they feel that someone else's ideas are better than theirs, they would start humiliating that person. They would call their idea pointless and stupid.

- **Seductive Narcissist**

These types of narcissists are very cunning and try to manipulate others for their benefit. They use alluring and seductive ways to attract someone to them. Once they are attracted, they use that person for their own needs and desires. The main aim of such narcissists is to gain what they want from the other person. This could be compliments, gifts, love, or even attention. They have excellent skills in developing a connection with other people and keeping them close.

Scenario

In a social gathering, many people interact with one another. Everyone is making friends with everyone, and a positive environment is experienced.

Normal Person's Reaction:

You would enjoy the company and try to be friends with everyone. They won't be bothered by their class or wealth and will try to be friends with everyone.

A Seductive Narcissist's Reaction:

A seductive narcissist, on the other hand, would go for the person who is the wealthiest among all. They would try to flirt with them and make a special connection. As narcissists always think of themselves as unique and special, they won't be interested in everyone. They would only use flattery and charming tactics with the person they want to benefit from

- **Narcissist Parent**

Such type of narcissists use their children to portray a good image of them. They often have unrealistic expectations from their children. They expect them to be more attractive, intelligent, and successful than all the other children. They never care about their children's well-being or emotions and just put unbearable duties on them. They feed their egos by showing their child's achievements in front of the world.

Scenario

It is time for a child to choose their career. They have just completed high school and are ready to enter a university.

Normal Parent's Reaction:

A normal parent would prioritize their children's interests and passions. They would make decisions that would keep their children at ease and would not go against their will.

A Narcissist Parent's Reaction:

A narcissistic parent would never keep their child's passion as the priority. They would force them to pursue a career that would keep their image in society. If they resist, the narcissistic parent might use emotional blackmailing, guilt, and manipulation to get what they want.

- **Grandiose Narcissist**

These are the narcissists who believe that they are the most exceptional human beings on this Earth. They have a worth that is higher than all the others. They constantly want people to admire and praise them. They always demand special care and treatment and get assertive if they lack any.

Scenario

A department assembly is being conducted where everyone talks about their achievements for this year.

Normal Person's Reaction:

A normal person would tell about their achievements and emphasize teamwork and efforts. They would also give thanks to everyone who contributed to their achievements. They would simply take a minute or two to end their speech.

Grandiose Narcissist's Reaction:

A grandiose narcissist would start by telling everyone how successful this year had been for them. They would go on and on, simply discussing their achievements and never giving attention to anyone else. They would exaggerate their achievements and shadow everyone else's work. They would boast about themselves and belittle anyone questioning or pointing them.

- **Know-it-All Narcissist**

These types of narcissists want people to think of them as the wisest and most intelligent of all. They make people feel as if they have knowledge regarding every topic and would dismiss the opinions of others if they try to interfere. They want to force intellectual dominance on others and maintain a good reputation.

Scenario

A team meeting is happening, and everyone is participating and expressing their ideas on the "impacts of greenhouse gasses on the climate."

Normal Person's Reaction:

An average person would also express their views and respect other people's opinions. They would understand if another person disagrees with them and would never make a fuss about it.

A Know-it-all Narcissist's Reaction:

This type of person would create an imbalanced discussion and try to degrade other people's views. They would be unable to bear any criticism and start rejecting others' ideas.

- **Self-Righteous Narcissist**

These are the types of narcissists who think that their values and morals are the best. They believe that no one can question or judge them. On the other hand, they judge other people's values and morals and see them as inferior. They try to preach to everyone about their learning and display themselves as the highest authority.

Scenario

A family dinner and various foods are going on. There is food for vegetarians as well as non-vegetarians.

Normal Person's Reaction:

An average person respects everyone's choices and avoids any debate. They would not cause any disputes and enjoy dinner with everyone.

A Self-Righteous Narcissist's Reaction:

Self-righteous narcissists would start lecturing everyone on table manners and criticize the ones who eat non-vegetarian food. They would create a hostile environment and spoil the family dinner.

- **Vindictive Narcissists**

These are the types of narcissists that hold grudges and take revenge. If someone does them wrong, they will go to great lengths to destroy his lives. They feel that the person has hurt their ego and view them as a threat.

Scenario

A person fights with another person in the office. Both had a minor disagreement, which led to a quarrel.

Normal Person's Reaction:

A normal person would forget about the incident after some time. They might forgive the other person and move on. They would resolve the conflict and, if necessary, seek support from HR.

Vindictive Narcissist's Reaction:

A Vindictive narcissist would start spreading rumors about the other person and would do anything to harm their reputation. They would also degrade them in front of others and assert useless power.

- **Addictive Narcissist**

These types of narcissists are much indulged in their pleasure. They do not think a situation would harm another person; they only think of themselves. They indulge in dangerous situations like drug use, spending a lot of money, or adventures that would boost their image. Their relationships are unstable and have a lot of problems.

Scenario

A couple is going through a financial crisis. They do not have enough money in their bank and are planning their finances.

Normal Person's Reaction:

A normal person would be considerate of their partner's worries and plan maturely. They would focus on important things like groceries, bills, and other stuff. They would cut out all unnecessary finances like shopping, etc.

Addictive Narcissist's Reaction:

Addictive narcissists would keep those things as a priority that pleases them. They would ignore all the other things like bills, etc., and would make shopping or drugs their priority. They would not care if their partner would suffer and be worried. They would never cut off expenses that bring them happiness.

The Ripple Effect: How Narcissism Affects Connections

The long-lasting impacts of being in a narcissistic relationship are far more than you can imagine. Narcissism not only impacts you as an individual itself but also cripples the lives of those around you. It causes an impact on the narcissistic family, partner, friends, social circle, and even their professional life.

The road to becoming a better person and healing is quite bumpy. Still, if you have the proper determination, you will succeed. Remember that your loved ones deserve love, peace, and, above all, respect. It is time to realize the sacrifices that your friends and family have made to protect you and understand your mental health.

Imagine a mother who, to the outside world, is the perfect example of motherhood. She speaks softly, showers her children with love, and is credited for their achievements. But behind closed doors, she changes. She yells at her husband and kids for anything that displeases her. This stark contrast between her public grace and private harshness reveals a profoundly emotional and complex reality.

We all have been abused in our childhood to some extent. And I know that this emotional baggage is burdensome to carry. However, the children who grew up in a narcissistic environment have baggage that is the heaviest of all. They grow to become narcissists themselves and spend their lives hiding their insecurities and trauma. They have been a victim of extreme criticism and manipulation and treated with a lack of empathy.

A person suffering from NPD experiences extreme negativity and always feels inadequate. They feel as if they are not of much worth and thus fall into depression. They often undergo excessive anxiety attacks and become sensitive to their emotions. They have low self-esteem and always try to cover this up through toxic tactics and behaviors. If you have narcissistic tendencies in your behavior, you can get an idea of how your relationships can be affected in different roles.

Effects of Narcissism on Various Relationships

• Parents

Sarah is the eldest child of her parents and suffers from narcissism. She constantly criticizes her parents and dulls the spark of her relationship with them. Whenever she fails, she blames her parents and questions their upbringing. Although her parents do their best to support her emotionally, they still feel as if they have never done enough.

If you sincerely look into this situation, you will realize that soon Sarah's parents would develop a mental health condition. The manipulation and guilt would build up, leading to depression. Sarah reduces her parents to tears with her constant criticism and harsh words. If this continues, eventually, her parents will withdraw from social gatherings and end their friendships. This is because Sarah's words would have made them question their worth. This negative situation might pass onto generational cycles and harm them.

• Siblings

Sam is an elder brother who is a sight for the sore eyes. Besides being charming, his intelligence is also unmatchable. On the other hand, Brian is the youngest brother. Besides his incredible football skills, he could be better at studying. He spends most of his time playing football or watching FIFA on the TV. Sam, being a narcissist, compares his grades with Brian and belittles him. They start to develop an unhealthy and deep rivalry. Brian begins to feel humiliated and develops insecurities. Sam tries to dominate Brian in every decision and control his life. This has created a hostile environment in the home and their lives.

If this situation persists, soon Brian will fall to psychological issues and become emotionally unstable. He might lose his interest in football and any other passion that he might have. He would feel inadequate and believe he doesn't deserve any success. He might start feeling jealous of his elder brother and try to harm him.

The family also suffers due to this situation. Brian starts to avoid family gatherings, so Sam does not humiliate him in front of everyone. Communication between family members is reduced, and they become distant.

In the future, Brian may develop defensive behavior and try to blame other people. He will never accept his mistakes and will destroy his relationships with everyone. He will not live a normal, healthy life, and will become overly conscious of himself.

- **Friends**

Chris has always been the center of the group's attention. Everyone loves him because of his charm and leadership qualities. However, with time, all of his friends start to realize a shift in Chris' behavior. He never lets anyone else take the spotlight and start to degrade other people. He starts to humiliate others in the name of jokes. If anyone tries to question him, he becomes defensive and aggressive.

As time passes, all of his friends start to keep a distance from him. They become afraid to share any secrets with him as he becomes unreliable. They are afraid to open up to him and always sugarcoat their real feelings. This is because they are worried about creating a negative environment by triggering Chris' insecurities. They will start to hang out without him and avoid all the drama and tension that Chris causes.

Chris also dismisses the achievements of others, which might cause other friends to doubt their abilities. Chris makes them feel as if they are unimportant and do not deserve respect. Chris's narcissistic reactions lead to the breakdown of trust, love, and friendship. They start to breach each other's trust and destroy their relations. They may isolate Chris from the friend circle, which would further worsen Chris' attitude and behaviors.

- **Partners**

Diana's relationship with Gary starts to cripple when her constant need for validation starts to overwhelm her. This has created an imbalance in her relationship and led to emotional exhaustion for both partners.

Diana constantly manipulates Gary for her needs and never acknowledges his efforts. Gary starts to feel neglected and struggles with mental well-being.

If Diana continues to act this way, Gary will start to doubt her feelings for him. He would become overly conscious about his actions and remain in a continuous state of stress and anxiety. Other women could easily trap him if his emotional needs are not met. In a relationship, it is essential that the needs of both partners are met and they both have respect for each other.

But, in the case of Diana and Gary's relationship, Diana always starts to make a fuss about Gary's needs and manipulates him into thinking that they are not worth it. This emotional abuse by Diana could make Gary weak and susceptible to mental illnesses.

He feels demotivated to work and needs more in his professional life. He has a hard time concentrating and gets exhausted quickly.

There are many chances that this relationship will break up, and both of the hearts will suffer. This will lead to a cycle of loneliness and regret.

- **Academic Life**

Monica is a super-talented student and always gets the highest grades in class. She leads her group projects and maintains a good reputation in front of everyone. However, her narcissistic traits start to show up when another girl named Stella gets admitted to her class. Stella is also a bright student and teachers love her intellectual answers.

Monica starts to feel insecure and tries to bring Stella down whenever possible. She spreads rumors about her and neglects her opinions. Monica also starts to act dominantly and tries to control everyone around her, creating an uncooperative environment in the class.

If Monica continues to act this way, then the class discipline will be disturbed. Teachers will start noticing student behavior changes and may become strict. The students will need more understanding or cooperation with one another. They will begin to avoid working with Monica and end their friendship with her. They will also cut terms with Stella due to the rumors that have been spread. This will destroy the unity of the class, leading to social isolation. Students will no longer participate in the discussions positively. Stella will resist expressing her views on a topic as she might fear humiliation.

Soon, everyone will notice Monica's behavior and uncontrollable dominance. They might discuss it with the teachers or the principal, which might lead to Monica being expelled. Teachers will no longer be happy with Monica, and this would give her constant stress and anxiety. Her mental condition would worsen, leading to many more psychological issues.

- **Personal Life**

Noah's narcissistic traits are triggered by his excessive use of social media. He constantly needs admiration and validation from others. If he uploads a picture, he spends all day staring at it or reading the comments again and again. He scrolls through Instagram all day long, comparing his life to those of the influencers.

If this continues, Noah will develop a sense of low self-esteem and suffer from his own insecurities. His mind will never allow him to be satisfied with what he has and will always focus on what he doesn't have. His relationships will start to suffer, and his close ones might become distant from him. He will always try to portray himself as a perfectionist so that people will admire him.

Soon, he will not be able to hear any constructive criticism. His emotions and self-being would get damaged, and he would go through many underlying issues. His mental health, self-growth, and his relationships will not be stable.

Manipulative Behaviors and Relationship Instability

People who suffer from narcissistic disorder manipulate others by using tactics that would help them to mold the situations to their own benefit. Eventually, these manipulation techniques will leave the other person isolated and in doubt.

Let's have a look at some techniques that you as a narcissist may use to manipulate others consciously or unconsciously:

1. Gaslighting

Gaslighting is a technique that narcissists use to gain control over the minds of others. In this technique, the narcissist makes other people question their thoughts and memories. They try to hide the reality and trick them into thinking that something didn't happen. They may play tricks with others' minds by blaming the mistake on them or trying to change the facts, leaving them confused and in despair.

2. Blame Game

Trying to act as a victim is another technique that narcissists use to manipulate another person. In this technique, the narcissist acts as a victim and makes the other person feel as if they are suffering because of their behaviors. Although narcissists might have initiated the conflict, they would exaggerate the situation and make everyone feel as if they were going through an intense time. They do not take responsibility for their actions and always blame the other person.

3. Projection

Narcissists always project their security onto others. For instance, if a narcissist is insecure about cheating, then they might accuse their partner of it. Accusing the other partner acts as a shield to hide their insecurities.

4. Isolation

A narcissist would always try to isolate others so they could take control over them more easily. Another person is an easy target for them when they know no one is beside them. They might start turning them against their family and friends by talking wrong about them or even asking them never to meet them again.

5. Lack of Emotions

Narcissists do not positively express their emotions, and this is one of the most common reasons why narcissistic relationships do not last long. For a relationship to flourish, both partners should have love and respect for each other. However, if a person is in a narcissistic relationship, then their partner will show no love and sympathy for them. Thus, the non-narcissistic person would end up sad and lonely.

How to Build Healthy Relations

It might be difficult to identify whether you are the problem in your relationship or the other person. This is because most of the time we are in a defensive state and fail to realize our mistakes. We assume that by making mistakes, our perfectionism would be questioned. People would start to target us and blame everything on us.

However, it is important to make genuine connections based on loyalty and trust. Thus, here is a group of worksheets that are specially designed for you. They help you to identify the areas in your relationship where you lack and help you to improve them.

The Compliment Challenge

Follow the instructions below to carry out this activity.

Instructions:

1. Prepare yourself for a challenge. Decide on a time frame in which you will notice positive things about people.
2. Once you have noted the positive things, you will compliment these people with a genuine heart.
3. At the end of the day, write down each compliment that you gave in the worksheet below.

My Complimentary Diary

Person1: ____

Person2: ____

Person3: ____

Person4 ____

Person5: ____

Relationship Vision Board

This activity will help you to manifest love and kindness in your relationship and strengthen them.

Instructions:

1. Cut out a large piece of cardboard by using scissors.
2. Now, collect various pictures, stickers and magazines.
3. Start visualizing the type of relationships that you want to have with your loved ones.
4. Paste the pictures or stickers that relate to your vision on the piece of cardboard.

Tada! You have now created your own vision board!

Place it where you can see it daily. Your mind will automatically start acting in the way your vision board wants it to act.

Peep into the Mind of a Narcissist

Let's dive deeper into the mind of a narcissist and see what the psychologists have to say regarding them! This chapter will allow you to understand the reason behind your narcissistic behaviors and reactions. This part will walk you through the most famous theories of narcissism. It will tell you about all the real-life stories of narcissists and how they overcame their fears! It will surprise, motivate, and prepare you to deal with your narcissistic tendencies for the future simultaneously.

So, let's take a jump into the world of the theories!

Psychological Theories of Narcissism

1. The Narcissistic Personality Inventory (NPI)

Question: Have you ever wanted to be the center of attention a little too much?

Let's Explore: Imagine being at a party where everyone is gathered around you, listening to your story.

It feels great to be the show's star. Do you feel insecure when someone else gets this attention? Do you always desire to be in the spotlight?

This is due to the Narcissistic Personality Inventory (NPI). Psychologists Robert Raskin and Calvin S. Hall wanted a technique to measure narcissism. Thus, they created a tool called the NPI. It is used to assess the traits related to narcissism, which include leadership and self-centeredness. This tool is similar to a personality quiz but has a higher purpose.

This NPI helps differentiate between self-confidence and self-centeredness. It has a variety of questions that help us understand how people perceive themselves. By looking at the participants' answers, psychologists can determine the level of narcissism in a person. This tool allows us to gain a deeper understanding of narcissism and how it impacts everyone.

2. The Dark Triad

Question: Do you have someone in your friend circle who is extremely charming but makes you feel uncomfortable?

Let's Explore: Think about a time when you were at a gathering and you met someone with an attractive personality. However, as you spent time with them, you felt uneasy. Did you realize what was wrong with them?

Psychologists Delroy Paulhus and Kevil Williams introduced us to the concept of the 'Dark Triad'. This is a combination of three personality traits, including the following:

- Narcissism
- Machiavellianism
- Psychopathy

To understand this concept, think of a ven diagram. In this diagram, these three personalities overlap and create a single personality. Now this single personality is far more dangerous than all three of them.

In such a personality, the narcissism trait would make the person crave self-admiration. The Machiavellianism would make them act in a manipulative and cunning way. Psychopathy would add a lack of empathy to them.

The triad dark helps us to recognize the cunningness and uncaring behaviors that hide behind a charming mask.

3. Object Relations Theory

Question: Do you feel as if your childhood experiences still have an impact on you and your personality?

Let's Explore: Think of your childhood memories and try to remember the most memorable things. It could be a bad experience or a good one. How did it impact you and still does?

This concept is explained by Object Relations Theory. Melanie Klein and Donald Winnicott were two psychologists who developed this theory. It explains the impacts that our childhood experiences leave on us. They also shape our personality and affect the way we live our lives. The care and love given by your caregivers shape your future.

Object Relations Theory is of the view that a person who has a stable childhood will develop a healthy self-image. However, a person who has an abusive childhood will develop feelings of insecurity and have many fears. As a result, these individuals try to seek attention and validation from other people. This theory helps us to understand the behaviors of narcissistic people and the underlying issues behind them.

4. The Narcissistic Cycle

Question: Do you think you are happy at one moment and throwing tantrums the very next?

Let's explore: Try to remember when you had a very high sense of self one day and felt worthless the next. You experience everything on highs and lows and leave others wondering what is wrong with you.

This is referred to as the narcissistic cycle. It explains the extreme behaviors of people and how they shift between grandiose and vulnerable narcissists. When you are in the grandiosity phase, you think highly of yourselves and seek admiration. However, when you are in a vulnerable state, you feel worthless and inadequate.

Psychologists have discovered that such behavior is due to unstable self-esteem and image. The narcissists try to protect themselves from the feelings of extreme worthlessness. Thus, they go into the grandiosity phase. When this phase ends, they again develop feelings of inadequacy and become highly insecure.

5. Vulnerable vs. Grandiose Narcissism

Question: Have you ever noticed how you can flip from feeling like you're on top of the world one day to feeling incredibly insecure the next?

Let's Explore: Do you swing between being super confident and then suddenly, really vulnerable? Have you ever wondered why your mood or behavior can change so drastically?

This is where we get into the idea of vulnerable vs. grandiose narcissism. Psychologists have figured out that narcissism isn't just one thing—it actually comes in two very different forms. Vulnerable narcissists are usually sensitive and often keep their insecurities hidden. They want to be admired, but even the smallest criticism can really get to them. On the other hand, grandiose narcissists are the complete opposite—they're bold, loud, and believe they're incredibly important.

These two sides show how the same need for validation can look totally different. A vulnerable narcissist might come across as shy and reserved, while a grandiose narcissist is more likely to be the life of the party, always in the spotlight. By understanding these differences, you can get a clearer idea of how narcissistic traits shape the way you act and interact with others.

6. Freud's Seminal Paper on Narcissism

Sigmund Freud wrote a paper on narcissism in 1915, where he explained the difference between primary narcissism and secondary narcissism. Now, primary narcissism is one of the most essential stages in the development of a child's self-esteem. Children are unaware of the hardships and difficulties of life and live in their carefree world. They know their parents are always there to protect and provide for them. They take their first steps with the belief that their parents won't let them fall. They believe that the world revolves around them and they are the main characters in everyone's lives.

The problem occurs when a child becomes so obsessed with this fantasy that it gets extended to adulthood. The child fails to realize the difference between fantasy and reality. They believe whatever they think or want is truth, and everything else doesn't matter. They become the center of attention and possessive if someone else tries to steal it. To understand this concept, you need to think of a baby. Babies are always said to be self-centered. They cry when they want food, need to sleep, or want their parents' love. Now, we would never call babies selfish. We know that it's just a part of their survival mode.

Similarly, a selfish person may also want admiration and attention from others. They may post daily on social media to gain this attention and be hungry for likes and comments. Freud believes that when a person grows, their validation is redirected, and they crave it from others. Freud's paper on narcissism shows how complex self-love can become and how it can become dangerous if not appropriately balanced.

Narcissistic Characters in Media

Disney has been telling magical tales to children for many years. However, the animated joy holds deep secrets of sadness and depression. Children watch their favorite cartoons endlessly only to grow up and understand the underlying meanings the cartoons have. Whether be it, *Ariel,* with her obsessive-compulsive disorder, or *Piglet,* going on anxiety-ridden adventures. Disney has always made us realize that we should look deeper into things.

A perfect example of a cartoon character showing narcissistic personality disorder is the evil queen from *Snow White and the Seven Dwarfs.*

She had deep-rooted insecurities that she wanted to hide. When she used to ask the mirror who was the fairest of them all, the mirror provided her name. This satisfied her ego and boosted her self-esteem. However, when the mirror once replied with the name of snow white, the queen felt deeply insecure. She became so threatened that she even decided to kill snow white. This shows that the queen was so self-absorbed that she had no empathy for anyone.

Let's have a closer look at the character of Scar, the villain brother of Mufasa, in The *Lion King.* He wanted to take control of everyone around him. This need to take power over everything led to Scar killing his brother and targeting his nephew Simba.

Another perfect example of NPD can be seen in Gaston from *Beauty and the Beast.* He thinks of himself as the town's most handsome, charming, and intelligent person. From lacking empathy to seeking validation from other people, Gaston possessed all the symptoms of narcissistic personality disorder. He never respected or cared about another person and even treated his best friend horribly. He even sang a song in the movie titled "Me," which depicted how self-obsessed he was. Throughout the movie, he disregards other people's feelings and opinions.

Chapter 3: Roots of Narcissism; Unearthing the Source

This chapter is all about digging deep into the roots of narcissism. Let's wander into the forest of narcissism and find out how different factors shape our personalities. These factors may be present in the past or we may be experiencing them in the present. We will explore various branches of this forest from childhood experiences to biological factors and many more! This chapter is all about identifying the underlying issues that cause you to act in a narcissistic way. Through this chapter, you will gain a true understanding of yourself. It will help you to be better equipped to deal with your fears and insecurities.

Let's get started!

Why Do We Become Narcissists?

To become a better person, you must understand the hidden meanings of your behaviors. Sometimes, a person acts in a toxic way because there are so many underlying issues that they fail to see. Similarly, to let go of narcissistic traits, one has to know the truth behind their narcissism. The roots of narcissism are a complex mixture of psychological, environmental and biological factors. It is time that we explore these roots and break free from them!

Psychological Origins

Have you ever felt that some personality traits are so deeply embedded within you that it nearly seems impossible to leave them?

Freud's discovery of narcissism can help us understand the psychological origins of narcissism. As we have already learnt before, there are two types of narcissism: primary narcissism and secondary narcissism.

When a child is in the infant stage, they want all the attention and care. This helps them survive and fulfil their sleep, food, and comfort needs. As the child grows up, they start to shift their sense of love towards other people. In this way, they express their love and affection to their parents or siblings. This creates balance and harmony in their lives and makes them aware of reality.

However, if a child does not grow to shift the sense of love towards others and keep it directed towards them, they get entangled in the chains of narcissism. Giving proper attention and love to the children is essential so they grow up under normal conditions.

This shows that narcissism is a natural stage of development. However, if there are any complexities in this stage of development, then the child might develop narcissistic personality disorder. The complexities may arise from providing inconsistent emotional support to the children. As a result, a fragile ego in the child is created that requires constant validation from others to feel supported and satisfied. Over time, this need grows and develops into narcissistic traits that kill relationships and destroy the peace of life.

Through Freud's discovery of narcissism, we also get to know that different types of complexities result in various kinds of narcissistic personalities. For instance, some narcissists are referred to as vulnerable narcissists and others are referred to as grandiose narcissists. However, the internal struggle of most narcissists is the same, and they go through the same feelings of inadequacy.

Freud's work on narcissism set the ground for many more discoveries on narcissism. He helped us understand the basic concept behind narcissism and how it is not a toxic behavior but a personality disorder. Just like other disorders, narcissistic personality disorder should also be treated with kindness and taken seriously.

Impacts of Childhood Experiences

Have you ever felt that you learned so much from your childhood experiences that you cannot unlearn now?

Childhood experiences mainly influence narcissistic traits. Our caregivers' love and support, whether parents or siblings, leave the most lasting impacts on our brains. It has been proven by research that narcissistic traits often develop from extreme conditions of either excessive love or neglect. A study by Brummelman, Thomaes, and Sedikides in 2021 suggests that both parental overvaluation and neglect can significantly contribute to the formation of these traits. If a parent showers a child with extra love and care, they might be cut off from reality and start living in their own fantasy world. In their fantasy world, they would be the most critical person in the room, everyone would fulfil all their needs, and nobody compares to them.

For instance, if a parent constantly reminds their child of their superior abilities and excessively praises them, the child will start to feel a sense of entitlement and superiority over others. They will exhibit the same beliefs in real life and show strong dominance in their relationships.

Similarly, a child who experiences extreme neglect from their parents adopts narcissistic traits as their self-defense mechanism. Suppose a parent constantly compares a child with his other siblings and makes them feel as if they are unimportant. In that case, the child develops insecurities and low self-esteem.

The tactic of the scapegoat child and the golden child can help you better understand this concept! Many parents use this controlling technique to manipulate their children into maintaining the family's reputation.

In this technique, the parents compare a child (scapegoat child) with another sibling (golden child) higher in intellect or beauty. They put all the blame on the scapegoat child and made the golden child their favorite. This manipulation technique makes the scapegoat child jealous and insecure of the other sibling. They start to develop insecurities that they try to hide by showing excessive dominance, stealing all the attention, or constantly talking about themselves. The other people fail to realize the battles that the scapegoat child is fighting alone and label them as "narcissists".

You might think that the golden child is at a better end. But, if you look closely, you might realize the manipulation they face daily. When a parent compares the scapegoat child with the golden child, the golden child is unintentionally burdened with the responsibility of keeping the family's image and reputation. They must always keep their interests and passion aside and follow whatever their parents tell them.

Genetic and Biological Factors

Do you feel that some of the toxic behaviors you show are inherited and there is nothing you can do about it?

Like your eye color or height, some aspects of your personality can be influenced by genetics. Research shows that our genetic makeup plays a role in shaping our personality traits, including those linked to narcissism. For instance, studies on twins reveal that identical twins often exhibit similar levels of narcissism, more so than fraternal twins, suggesting a genetic component to the disorder. A recent study by Crowe, Shryack, and Miller in 2022 supports this, highlighting the genetic influences on narcissistic traits through twin studies and genetic analyses.

The variations in different parts of the brain also have an impact on the personality of a person. Narcissistic people have a prefrontal cortex and amygdala that is different from other people. These brain parts are involved in self-regulation, empathy, and emotional processing. As a result, people with narcissism find it difficult to empathize and feel for others.

The prefrontal cortex is responsible for making decisions and controlling one's reactions. Narcissistic people thus behave impulsively and recklessly. Their prefrontal cortex shows reduced activity.

The amygdala is responsible for processing emotions. Selfish people have an underdeveloped amygdala and thus react unusually to certain situations.

Neurotransmitters are the chemicals responsible for transmitting signals between the brain and different parts of the body. These chemicals also impact our mood and how we experience happiness. For instance, an overactive dopamine system will cause a person to feel a greater need for admiration and validation. As a result, these individuals are mostly found trying to get validation from others.

Understanding these genetic and biological factors gives us a more rounded view of narcissism. It shows that our environment doesn't just shape narcissistic traits but is also deeply rooted in our biology. Recognizing this can help us approach narcissistic personality disorder with more empathy, realizing that factors beyond our control influence our behaviors.

Parenting Style and Influence

A child's upbringing plays a vital role in developing their personality. There needs to be a balance between love and authority. If parents show any excess of these, it may lead to a damaged personality.

Parents who are carefree and show excessive love to their children may negatively influence them. On the other hand, parents who show excessive dominance grow up with children rooted in deep insecurities.

A parenting style that balances love and dominance grows children with the healthiest self-image and mental well-being. They live their lives in balance and always approach them positively. They care for the people around them and treat them with respect.

Parents who show excessive dominance over their children destroy their mental well-being. They grow up narcissists who are highly insecure and have self-doubt. For instance, if a child grows up in a family where love is given only under a condition, the child will develop fears. To hide these fears and insecurities, he will act selfishly. He will crave validation and attention from the other people.

Parents who show excessive love and care also bring up narcissistic children. The children show a high sense of them and thus treat others with disrespect. For instance, a child grows up in a household where he can do anything he wants without seeking permission. This child will develop unrealistic expectations and get disturbed in the real world. They will do anything without fearing the consequences. Such behavior is not tolerated in the real world, and the child may be termed a narcissist.

Parents should always maintain a balance in their parenting style and be considerate of their children's well-being and emotions.

Role of Trauma and Abuse

Have you ever felt that your behaviors are influenced by the trauma that you faced in your life?

NPD in a person can also be influenced by trauma and abuse that they had faced in the past. People who have gone through psychological, emotional or physical assault develop narcissistic traits to hide the scars from these traumas. This abuse has a strong effect on their brains that creates a sense of low self-esteem in the individuals.

When a child goes through trauma, they experience a rush of overwhelming emotions. To control these emotions, they develop defense mechanisms for themselves. These defense mechanisms may end up as grandiosity, narcissistic traits, and a need to control everything. These individuals in the past were deprived of control and power. Thus they exhibit an excess of them when they grow up. This unnecessary control and dominance help the traumatized individuals hide their feelings of helplessness and fear.

For instance, if a child experiences bullying or abuse, they will show extreme dominance and control when they grow up. This gives them a feeling of satisfaction and relief that everything will go according to their will. This grandiose self-image creates a safe place for them and helps them forget their traumas.

Also, people who have gone through emotional trauma and abuse find it hard to trust others. They are not able to develop meaningful relationships and thus lack emotional support. They try to maintain relations with those people who would boost their self-image and self-esteem.

Individuals who have narcissistic personality disorder have deep-seated pain and insecurities that force them to act in toxic ways. Although healing from trauma demands significant courage, it ultimately frees you from the toxicities in your life.

Social and Cultural Influence

Social and cultural influences can enhance narcissistic traits. Social media plays a significant role in developing narcissistic personalities. In today's world, excessive use of social media pressures individuals to maintain a perfect image in front of the world. Such use leads to constant validation from others and a lack of self-confidence.

Social media platforms like Instagram, Facebook and TikTok allow people to compare themselves and their lives with celebrities and influencers. The influencers showcase a perfect body, a perfect life and a luxurious lifestyle, which negatively influences the brain. The person starts to compare their lives with those of the influencers, thus complaining and depressed. This creates a sense of low self-worth in them and, therefore, develops narcissistic traits in them. The world of social media has affected genuine connections, and all which is left is showing off and competing with each other.

Consumerism strongly promotes the idea that our worth is tied to what we own and how we look. Advertisements and media constantly show us images of a lifestyle filled with luxury, beauty, and success, making it seem like these are the ultimate goals in life. This message can make us believe that having more and better things will make us more valuable and respected.

Imagine seeing a commercial for the newest smartphone, with sleek visuals and celebrities using it effortlessly. Think about how getting the latest phone might make you feel like you're successful or important. That urge to keep up with everyone else can create a cycle where you always want the newest thing, and before you know it, you start to measure your worth by what you own.

Then there's the whole "hustle culture" idea. It's all about working non-stop, achieving more, and constantly promoting you. This mindset pushes us to put our careers and personal goals above everything else. It's about the grind, that next big win, and staying ahead.

How many times have you heard phrases like "rise and grind" or seen posts celebrating late-night work sessions? This constant pressure to succeed makes us so focused on our personal achievements that we sometimes forget about empathy and real connections. We get so caught up in the race to succeed that we lose sight of the importance of the people around us. When we understand how consumerism and hustle culture shape our thinking, it's easier to see why some people start to develop narcissistic traits. These cultural pressures can shape behaviors that prioritize self-image and success over meaningful connections.

Early Relationships and Attachment Styles

Psychologists John Bowlby and Mary Ainsworth investigated the impacts that childhood attachment styles have on personality traits. The love and care our parents and family provide influence how we behave and adopt certain traits.

The attachment style is formed by how the needs of a child are met. Suppose the caregivers provide constant love and support and immediately respond to the child's needs. In that case, the child's healthy self-esteem is built. This is referred to as the secure attachment and ensures the well-being of a person. The best example of such attachment is a household where the family members celebrate one another's achievements and provide emotional support. The members of this family will live a happy and balanced life. Their relationships and friendships will be genuine and strong.

However, suppose a person grows up in a household where the parents provide inconsistent care and love. In that case, the person might develop an anxious attachment. Such parents ignore their children, and children care for them when they have time. This makes the child question their worth, and thus, they totally become self-dependent. As a result, these individuals may appear confident and self-assured, but deep within, they hold insecurities. They do not form close connections with anyone and prefer to be alone. They also lack empathy and are very self-centered.

Children who grow up in inconsistent caregiving environments develop disorganized attachment styles. The parents of such children treat them as objects that will maintain their reputation. They do not express much love and care; thus, children develop fears deep inside them.

This chaotic relationship can leave a person feeling fragmented and unsure of who they are. As they grow up, they might swing between feeling overly confident—almost like they're on top of the world—and deeply insecure, questioning their worth. These intense shifts between highs and lows are standard in people with narcissistic personality disorder.

Media and Society's Impact

People tend to act like narcissists on social media as this gets them likes and comments. But it's important to recognize that our validation from a viral post is fleeting. Social media fuels our dependence on others' approval. We start craving their attention and positive feedback, but our sense of satisfaction needs to be improved. Once our moment in the spotlight fades, our self-esteem can quickly plummet to where it was before—or even lower down, especially if we've shared something personal.

This creates a vicious cycle. We find ourselves repeatedly engaging in these attention-seeking behaviors to get that quick hit of approval. For a brief moment, we might feel good about ourselves. Still, we will only know our worth if we keep receiving that instant and overwhelming validation. Over time, these behaviors can become habits and thus impact our lives and relations with others negatively.

Breaking Free from Narcissistic Roots

As you start this part of the book, please take a look back at your toxic behaviors and how they have caged you for so long. This chapter invites you to let yourself free from the cage of narcissism and live your life to the fullest. You will no longer indulge in self-doubt and isolation. This part is your key to experiencing a life full of positivity and happiness! With each step forward, you'll discover new strengths and possibilities, paving the way for a life that reflects your true self. This is your moment to shine, to break free from the shadows and step into the light of a brighter and more fulfilling future.

Diagnostic Criteria for Narcissistic Personality Disorder

As we mentioned at the start of the book, there is a difference between narcissistic traits and narcissistic personality disorder. Narcissistic traits are just behaviors that show uncontrollable dominance and self-admiration. At the same time, narcissistic personality disorder is a mental illness that causes emotional, physical, and cognitive disturbances. Narcissism can also be observed on a scale. At the one end of the scale is primary narcissism that everyone has. As we proceed further on the scale, narcissism starts to increase and soon develops into narcissistic personality disorder.

Narcissistic personality disorder influences you to act in a way that grabs everyone's importance or makes you feel necessary in everyone's eyes. Eventually, you become so used to these behaviors that they become a part of your personality. Narcissistic personality disorder can vary from looks to wealth to intellect and even skills.

There is not a correct idea of the % of people that have narcissistic personality disorder. This is because those narcissists are also good at hiding their narcissism and not getting caught.

According to a survey by the Diagnostic and Statistical Manual of Mental Disorders (DSM-5), approximately 0.5% to 5 % of the people in the USA have a narcissistic personality disorder. However, NPD is most common in men due to increased agentic behaviors. Narcissism is driven by people having the urge to be dominant, succeed in life and show superiority. In our society, males show more of these traits, so the NDP is found more in men.

A narcissistic personality disorder is not complex to diagnose. A psychologist or a psychiatrist can diagnose NPD by simply talking to the patient. They could ask various questions regarding their lives or how they would act. This helps them to get a clear view of where the patient is standing.

The Diagnostic and Statistical Manual of Mental Disorders, fifth edition text revision (also known as the "DSM-5-TR™" or just "DSM-5®") has nine criteria. You have to possess a minimum of 5 of them to be diagnosed with NPD. NPD cannot be diagnosed using diagnostic, lab, or imaging tests.

NPD causes moderate or severe problems in some regions of personality trait functioning:

- **Self-direction** involves setting goals based on getting acceptance from others, setting unreasonable expectations to feel exceptional, or setting too low standards due to a sense of entitlement

- **Lack of Empathy** is the inability to understand or recognize the feelings and needs of others. It involves being overly attuned to others' reactions, but only when perceived as relevant to oneself. It also consists of overestimating or underestimating one's impact on others.
- **Lack of intimacy** describes relationships that are shallow and mainly used to boost self-esteem. In these relationships, there is little genuine interest in the other person's experiences, and the focus is primarily on personal gain, which limits real cooperation.

Self-Reflection and Assessment Tools

Now, you might be thinking that there are many chances that you have all of these narcissistic traits or are just curious whether you are a grandiose narcissist or a vulnerable one. You might also be thinking of the impacts that you had on your relationship and the hurt that you have caused others.

Do not worry; let's dive together into a world full of self-assessment tools and exercises. These exercises are meant to uncover the real you and see things below the surface. Let's get started and understand ourselves better!

1. The Mirror Challenge: Seeing Your True Reflection

Stand in front of a mirror with a clear mind. Take a few deep breaths and stare directly into your eyes. Try to focus entirely on yourself and not get distracted by the surroundings. Now, think of all those people who are related to you. Take their names individually, and then think deeply about how your behaviors have hurt them. Please put yourself in their shoes and then feel how they would have felt.

Also, ask yourself questions about your relationships with your close ones. Do you have a secure, genuine connection with them, or do you have them for constant validation?

Keep all of your guard down and give yourself an honest answer. This activity is not about just seeing yourself in the mirror but a wake-up call to accept reality.

2. The Narcissism Scorecard: Where Do You Stand?

Find the Narcissistic Personality Inventory (NPI) quiz on your laptop. Go to a quiet and comfortable place where you won't be disturbed. Take the quiz with full attention and honesty.

You will find 40 statements and you have to choose the answers that match your personality the most. This activity takes around 5 to 10 minutes and helps you to identify the toxic and narcissistic traits within yourself. Analyze the results that it shows you and try to accept them instead of running away from the blame.

Understanding yourself will open new doors for self-improvement and growth. This quiz is the first step towards your road to healing. So, take it with complete honesty and self-acceptance.

3. My Ego Journal

You might have heard the benefits that keeping a journal brings. Journaling is a technique that helps you analyze things deeply and make your mind more straightforward. Now, keep a journal for yourself where you note down every situation in which you showed narcissistic traits. They might be controlling someone else's life, degrading someone, or even seeking validation from others.

At the end of the week, review all your behaviors and ask yourself the following questions:

- *What triggered me to act this way?*
- *What was I thinking when I reacted this way?*
- *Were there any other ways in which I could have responded?*

Keeping an ego journal will help you identify the toxic ways you behave and get to the core of them. You will be able to differentiate between reacting and responding to a situation. This will also help you to keep a record of your improvement and motivate you to become even better!

4. The Empathy Experiment: A Day in Their Shoes

In this activity, you will pick someone that you do not like or have bad connections with. You will spend a day looking at the world through that person's eyes. You will react the same way they respond to situations and then try to understand their point of view. You will write down all the experience on paper. Write down all the struggles, feelings, and thoughts that you went through while being in their shoes for a day.

This activity is meant to enhance your relations with others and build a sense of empathy. By considering others' points of view, you will start to react more calmly and understand their reactions.

5. The Conversation Balancer: Are You a Talker or a Listener?

As you know, one of the most common traits of narcissism is that narcissists constantly talk about themselves. So, for a week, note how much you have tried to steal the spotlight. Remember when you cut off the other person to discuss your achievements or success. At the end of the week, analyze the situation and see if you are a good listener or talker.

This activity helps you understand the importance of listening to others. It will also help you maintain a perfect balance of sharing, caring, and showing respect to others! You will form genuine connections with your friends and family and have boosted emotional support.

6. The Origin Story: Mapping Your Narcissistic Roots

Now, this is one of the most critical activities in this section. If you learn about the underlying issues of toxic behaviors, there are increased chances of ending them. In this activity, you will take a pen and paper and recall when you think your self-esteem got hurt. Write down every detail you remember, like your feelings at that time, or was there someone to help you? Reflect on the lasting impacts those moments had on you and your personality.

This activity is best carried out in the presence of a close friend or loved one, as it may evoke past traumas and could potentially lead to feelings of depression. This activity will help you to understand yourself in the best possible way.

7. The Reality Mirror: Getting Honest Feedback

Narcissistic personality disorder makes it difficult for you to trust other people. However, there will be some friends who are close and want the best for you. Reach out to those friends and ask for their honest opinions regarding your behaviors. Ask them to explain in detail so that you can change with determination. Be open to criticism and understand their point of view. This activity will give you a complete understanding of yourself and help you to overcome your toxic traits. It will strengthen your relationship with your close ones and help you live a happier life!

8. The Narcissism Type Quiz: Discover Your Style

Gain knowledge regarding different types of narcissism, including overt, covert, communal, and malignant. Try to observe these traits and reflect on which are present the most in you. Reflect on the impacts these traits have on your relationships.

This activity is an opportunity to help you overcome your narcissistic traits and be open to self-growth. It helps you to improve your life positively.

Cultural Reflections and Debunking Myths

There is so much hatred and negativity in the people regarding the word "Narcissist". People assume these people do not have feelings and are the most selfish. People show no empathy towards them and think of them as bad people. However, we fail to realize that they are human beings suffering from traumas and fears.

If the world had a little more understanding, it would have become such a beautiful place to live in. People have developed several myths about narcissistic people and treat them according to those myths. Let's dive into some of these myths and break them so that we can show more compassion towards people suffering from mental disorders.

Myth 1: Narcissists Are in Love with Themselves

You might think that selfish people are simply self-obsessed and enamored with themselves, but that's a misconception. In reality, individuals who display greedy behavior often have deep-seated insecurities and various fears.

Imagine Anna, who speaks highly of herself and always boasts about her success and achievements. Judging her and thinking she is full of herself can be straightforward. However, you fail to realize that this is a self-defense mechanism she uses to hide her insecurities and inferiority complex. Remember that a superiority complex is always used to cover up an inferiority complex.

Myth 2: People with NPD Have No Empathy

People suffering from NPD indeed find it difficult to empathize with other people, but it is not entirely true. Narcissists only show empathy towards the people they are very close with. Their empathy is underdeveloped and thus is only seen in situations that align with their emotions and needs.

Think of Charles, who fails to notice that his friend is upset, but when he does, he goes out of the way to help him. Charles has a difficult time recognizing the emotions of others, but he does care about them.

Myth 3: They're Not Aware of Their Disorder

Many people are of the view that narcissistic people are not aware of their disorder and think that everything is fine with them. However, this is entirely false. They know they have unstable emotions and reactions that hurt other people. But, they are afraid to stand up to their insecurities and learn about their behaviors. They fear that acknowledging their mistakes will only ruin their lives and hurt their self-esteem.

Imagine Dean, who knows that he ends up hurting his loved ones and even breaking up with his girlfriend frequently. However, he fails to accept his mistakes because he fears they will only hurt his image. He cannot think of breaking his self-esteem and seeing the issues beneath. He finds it easier to put the blame on the other person and satisfy his ego.

Myth 4: Narcissists Are "Bad" People

The most common misconception is that narcissists are bad people, and everyone should stay away from them. Such myths only worsen the situation of a person and make them more depressed. Selfish people are only human beings who are suffering from silent battles and trying to hide their traumas and insecurities.

Imagine Linda, who seeks validation from others by constantly posting on social media and gaining attention. Now, people would call her an attention seeker or a narcissist, but the reality is completely different. She might have grown up in a household where her parents constantly criticized her looks or weight. As a result, she tries to cover her insecurities by gaining attention and validation from other people.

Motivational Letter for Positive Change

Dear Friend,

I know that you have come a long way from loneliness, self-doubts, fears and insecurities. It was never easy for you to suffer through Narcissistic Personality Disorder, and there are many silent battles that you fought alone. But do not worry now; you are not alone in this journey now; we are together.

I know you are tired of faking a strong and self-obsessed image in front of the world to hide your insecurities. Sometimes, you want to be vulnerable and speak what your heart wants, but you choose to fake this personality. You need to understand that the most vital thing you can do is to stand up to your fears, look them in the eye, and face them. Continue to hide your worries behind the wall of glorious personality.

Not everyone dares to take the right steps and make the right choices. You should be proud of yourself that you are trying to become a better person. Your approach towards a positive life reveals a lot about you!

I know you might find it hard at times to overcome your narcissistic traits, but remember that I am with you. You are not alone! You will soon be so self-confident that you will no longer crave validation from others.

Everyone would respect and love you. You will have genuine friendships and relationships based on trust and love. You will get to experience a life you have always dreamt of. It is time to let go of your insecurities and take control of your life.

I believe in you and know that you will make it through this healing journey of yours.

Section 2:
Brightening the Way, Healing Each Day

Chapter 4: Steer Your Life: Escape Narcissism's Strife

This chapter will allow you to prepare for change and build up some strength for it. It will lead you to a more fulfilling and positive life! This chapter will guide you toward the first step of your healing journey.

The Emotional Pause

It is essential to take a pause from everything and focus on yourself. You need to take a deep breath and shift your focus towards yourself. You need to silence your negative thoughts and empower positivity. This section of the book will help you realize your true potential and reflect on your negative traits.

Power of Silence

People often misunderstand silence as loneliness. Silence holds strength and power, whereas loneliness makes you depressed. Silence reveals a lot about a person and helps them to know themselves better. In today's generation, it is a rare occasion for us to sit in silence or be alone with ourselves.

You should take a moment to embrace silence and cut off all the noise and distractions from your life.

Here is an activity designed to embrace silence and learn about yourself.

- **Step 1:** Go to your comfort place where you feel at peace. It might be a space in your home where nobody interrupts you or a spot in the park where you feel most comfortable.

- **Step 2:** Set a timer on our phone for around 15 minutes. Start taking slow breaths and maintain your focus on your breathing. If any thoughts arise, do not push them away. Acknowledge those thoughts and then shift your focus back to your breathing.

- **Step 3:** As you embrace the silence, let your mind travel into the past. Think deeply about all the memories that come up to the surface. Let yourself feel all the emotions that arise from those memories. Allow yourself to be vulnerable while you are in this state.

- **Step 4:** As soon as the timer goes up, slowly return to reality. Write down everything you experienced in your journal and keep track of them.

- **Step 5:** At the end of the week, analyze all the journal entries and try to associate the traumas that shaped your narcissistic traits. You might look for repeated thoughts or patterns of thinking to determine the underlying issues.

Accepting and Admitting Your Weaknesses

Acceptance is the key to freeing yourself from all the traumas in your life. Sometimes, it is tough to accept certain things. But the sooner you accept the reality, the better. It seems impossible for a selfish person to admit their mistakes. They have always lived up to the fantasy that they are perfect and have no flaws. However, accepting your flaws and reality is critical for self-growth.

Accepting that you can also make mistakes is not something you should be ashamed of. It just means that you have some areas in you that need improvement. It takes strength and courage to admit your mistakes and acknowledge that you hurt others with your actions. It is also widespread that stress from childhood can cause you to express anger, rage, and resentment. In the case of narcissism, traumatic stress can cause you to show dominance over other people and see them as inferior to you.

Here are a few ways to deal with the traumatic stress and not letting it control you.

- Allow yourself to express every emotion, whether sadness, shame, or anger. Sit with your pain and feel it completely.
- Be patient with your healing process and give it time.
- You need to feel everything deeply to let it go.
- You might experience emotions that will be difficult to deal with. Do not be hard on yourself and feel them completely.

Here is an activity designed to help you accept yourself and your emotions.

- **Step 1:** Stand quietly in front of a mirror and look directly into your eyes.
- **Step 2:** While looking deeply into your eyes, start acknowledging that you have hurt people from your narcissistic behaviors and traits.
- **Step 3:** Once acknowledged, promise to change for the better. Have faith in yourself that you will overcome all the negativity in life and break free from narcissism.

Preparing for Change

You are so brave for moving ahead on this self-healing journey! Take a moment to applaud yourself. Now, you are aware of the narcissistic traits in yourself. It is time to get rid of them and live a better life! This part of the book will help you to develop a special bond with your loved ones and change for the better!

Practicing Empathy

It might be challenging for a narcissistic person to experience empathy due to the habit of self-centeredness. However, it will help a narcissist to develop deeper connections and form friendships based on trust and love. Knowing you have people who really care for you gives you a purpose in life. Seeing the world through the eyes of other people allows you to understand their point of view. It makes you less selfish and lets you think of other people.

Here are a few steps that you can follow to practice empathy and create special bonds with your loved ones.

- **Step 1:** Go to a quiet place where nobody will disturb you. Now, recall a time when you kept your feelings and needs as a priority. Recall a time when you did not care about another person's feelings and did a thing that satisfied your needs.

- **Step 2:** Now, put yourself in the other person's shoes. Sincerely try to feel the emotions the other person would have felt then.

- **Step 3:** Write down all of this in a journal and then try to provide alternative ways in which you could have responded. Think of the ways that would have benefitted you both and met your needs.

- **Step 4:** Now make a firm resolution to avoid such behavior in similar situations in future.

Enhancing Communication Skills

Good communication skills are essential for living a meaningful and healthy life. Every person should learn to communicate their feelings in the best way possible. Narcissists always struggle with communication skills because they talk about themselves excessively. They always want to be the center of attention and thus feel insecure if it shifts towards someone else.

Narcissists need to become good listeners to develop good communication skills. They must realize that listening to another person's life does not make you look weak. It means you are considerate and compassionate enough to care for others and listen to what they say. This will help you create friendships based on mutual respect and love.

Here are a few ways to practice being a good listener with those around you.

- **Step 1:** When you are involved in a conversation, try to listen to what the other person has to say. After he has done the talking, you can share your response.

- **Step 2:** You should ask them more questions about the subject. This shows that you are interested and paying attention. It will also help you to gain a clear understanding of their perspective.
- **Step 3:** Once they have completed their conversation, try to summarize the conversation in simple words and provide genuine advice to them.
- **Step 4**: Try to understand their perspective and consider their suggestions and points of view too. Do not force them to only consider your point of view and suggestions. Don't give them the impression that you are the smartest person on the earth.

Resolving Conflicts Constructively

We will likely react rather than respond when we engage in a conflict. This is exceptionally true for people who have narcissistic personalities. They have built up traumas inside them, and getting into a conflict only triggers them more. As a result, their fight and flight responses in the body get activated. They would do anything to protect their self-esteem from getting harmed, whether it involves degrading the other person or spreading rumors about them.

Learning to resolve a conflict constructively and working through it is essential. This will make you respected in the eyes of other people, and they will stop involving themselves in unnecessary conflicts with you. Positively handling a conflict strengthens your relationships and does not damage anyone.

Here is a technique that might help you to resolve conflicts constructively.

- **Step 1:** Think of a situation in which you got involved in a conflict. Remember every detail of that conflict, including the reason that started it.

• **Step 2:** Ask a trusted friend or family member to act out the conflict. You will take turns representing both sides of the conflict. This will help you better understand the other person's behavior and the reasons behind the conflict.

• **Step 3:** Now, try to resolve this conflict by constructive resolution. Try to understand what the other person says and reasonably express your feelings. After this, try to find a compromise to satisfy you both.

Moving Away from Narcissistic Influence

Moving away from narcissistic influence means that you distance yourself from everything that would trigger you to act selfishly. This involves cutting off friends who hype you up to do bad things or deleting your social media accounts. To become a better person, you should befriend with the people who bring out the best in you. The environment in which you live plays a vital role in developing your personality. So, if you are trying to change, you should be around those with the same goals as yours.

The friends who want good for you will always try to encourage you towards your targets and always be there for you. They will consider your feelings and always give you positive advice. They also motivate you to make healthy choices if they are involved. These healthy choices can be as small as avoiding junk food or as big as giving up an argument. They will always try to push you towards a more positive life!

Here are a few steps that you should take to avoid narcissistic or negative influences in your life.

• **Step 1:** List all the people you meet in your daily routine, including your office and personal life. In front of their names, write the things or traits about them that trigger you the most. If nothing triggers you about a person, write about their traits that bring positivity to you.

• **Step 2:** Once you have listed the people you need to cut off, start making plans to avoid them. This might include changing your shift timings, taking another route while driving home, or simply not replying to their texts.

- **Step 3:** Replace these negative people with positive people in your life. You might carry out activities that promote personal growth and make you happy. Keep friends with people who encourage you to act in better ways and start doing some social work with them.

Rebuilding with Strength

It takes a lot of strength and courage to acknowledge your mistakes and try to become a better person. I am so proud of you for reading about your healing journey. Let's move forward and learn to build healthy self-esteem so that we can realize our worth. This section is all about building emotional resilience, practicing active listening skills and making our relationships better!

So, let's get started!

Building Healthy Self-Esteem

There is a thin line between ego and self-esteem. Having a healthy self-esteem allows you to live a positive and happier life. On the other hand, ego destroys all of your relationships and leaves you isolated. Self-esteem refers to accepting yourself and knowing you deserve love and respect.

It does not necessarily mean that you should be self-obsessed. It simply means that you know that even though you have flaws, you are still capable of love and care. Having healthy self-esteem allows individuals to be confident about themselves and the ideas or viewpoints they present. A person experiencing low self-esteem may not feel good about themselves and project their insecurities differently. It would help if you remember that nobody is perfect and everybody has flaws. Still, the real strength lies in overcoming your weaknesses and toxic behaviors. As a narcissist, you might have experienced situations where your self-esteem was threatened, or you did not feel secure. You need to realize the underlying issue that caused you to feel insecure.

Developing healthy self-esteem will not encourage aggressive and manipulative behavior. Instead, it will allow you to understand and resolve the situation logically like a mature person. You will be able to accept your mistakes and not play the blame game. This will help you preserve your relationships and form special bonds with your loved ones.

Here is an activity that can help you identify the areas in your personality that need improvement.

- **Step 1:** Just as you made an "Ego journal" initially, it is now time to make a "Self-Worth Journal". On the first page of the journal, write down a list of things you like about yourself. Focus on things that depict your inner self, not just your appearance.

- **Step 2:** In your journal, add the traits that you want to develop every day. Write down a positive affirmation for each trait and try to repeat it daily. For instance, if you want to develop patience, you can use the affirmation, "I am patient."

- **Step 3:** Repeat these affirmations daily as this will allow your brain to act automatically in the way you want it to.

Strengthening Active Listening Skills

In the previous section, you have learnt about effective communication and active listening skills. Now, let's have a look at them in more detail. Active listening skills are essential to maintain good communication between two people. It fosters relationships and develops a special bond between the people. Active listening skills can be a challenge for narcissists as they are self-centered. However, here are a few active listening skills that are easy to practice in the first place.

- Being mindful of the situation and avoiding distractions.

- Maintaining sound eye contact with the person speaking.

• Nodding your head when you agree on a point or using nonverbal cues.

• Asking questions related to the topic to improve the discussion.

• Never judge the other person's feelings and perspectives.

Here is an activity that can help you engage in meaningful conversations and practice active listening skills.

• **Step 1:** Talk about an issue your friend is currently facing.

• **Step 2:** Listen to them with full attention and try to practice active listening skills. Nod when you agree with their point and maintain good eye contact.

• **Step 3:** Try to reflect on their emotions and behaviors and provide them with emotional support and advice.

Building Emotional Resilience

Emotional resilience refers to the strength to encounter failures and defeat. It means getting back up once life knocks you down. Building solid emotional resilience is essential in managing your emotions and accepting reality. It allows you to face life's challenges with a clear mindset and makes you self-assured. Like emotional intellect, emotional resilience is also present in infants and continues to grow with age. However, situations or traumas in childhood might stunt the growth of emotional resilience, and thus, the child develops narcissistic traits. When a narcissist encounters a setback, they fail to accept it and make a big deal out of it. Their mind manipulates them to react in toxic ways which worsens the situation.

By developing solid emotional resilience, you can live a life of balance and satisfaction. Once you know you have given your best, you should leave the rest to the universe. You should firmly believe that if one door closes, another opens up.

Here is an activity that will help you develop emotional resilience and allow you to return after a setback.

- **Step 1:** Sit quietly and take a few deep breaths. Let your mind wander into the past and think of a situation where you were defeated. It can be as big as a breakup or as small as an argument. Now, think deeply about that situation and let all your feelings surface.
- **Step 2:** Write down all your feelings when you were defeated. Also, note down every reaction of yours, whether it was positive or negative.
- **Step 3:** Now, analyze your reactions and feelings and determine whether they were based on logic or sentiments. Write down alternative ways you could have reacted and maintained your positivity. Also, express your feelings about what you have learned from this experience.

Cultivating Inner Strength

We know the importance of focusing on mindfulness, meditation, self-confidence, etc. However, we need to know that inner peace lies in inner strength. It is the ability to face hardships with a smile on your face. It is about choosing the right path and making the right decisions, even if your heart breaks. It is the belief in yourself and your morals that they will stand still even if the world collapses. Finding your true inner strength is not a practice. Instead, it is a path you must follow—one that may be full of difficulties and hardships but with a beautiful destination.

Here is an activity that can help you gain inner strength and develop a deep connection with yourself.

- **Step 1:** Sit where no disturbances are present. Start breathing deeply and focus on your breaths.
- **Step 2:** As you take a deep breath, visualize a golden light shining out of your chest. Let this light fall onto your whole body and cover you in its peace.
- **Step 3**: Start repeating affirmations about the traits that you want to develop in yourself. Repeat words like "I am a good listener," and "I am strong".

- **Step 4:** Spend a few minutes in this state and then slowly start to come back into reality. Slow down your breathing and slowly open your eyes.

Building Healthier Relationships

Building relationships is very crucial for the survival of an individual. Relationships, whether with a partner or a friend, are beneficial for a person's mental well-being. People who are in a relationship or have genuine friendships experience less stress. They are aware of their partner or friends' social and emotional support. Moreover, having pure relationships can give a person a sense of purpose in their life. For example, many want to achieve something extraordinary to make their parents proud. Friends also drive you to be a better person and make the best out of your life. Whether you are stressed about your job or experiencing heartbreak, your friends will always cheer you up. A healthy relationship is one in which there is respect, love, and trust from both sides.

Here are a few ways to foster healthy relations and live a positive life!

1. Find Common Interests

It is essential to do activities that you both enjoy. In this way, you will be able to spend quality time with them and live a happy life. It can be as simple as joining an art class or cooking together.

2. Accept Your Mistakes

You need to accept your mistakes when you are wrong. Blaming the other person just damages the relationship and hurts them.

3. Be a Good Listener

You need to listen to the other person and be considerate about their thoughts and feelings. Listen to them with full attention and do not try to shift the conversation towards yourself.

4. Let Them Take Their Decisions

It is important to let everyone make their own decisions and not interfere too much in their lives. Do not try to manipulate other people to make choices that benefit you. Respect their feelings and give them space.

Chapter 5: The Journey Ahead: Embrace the Change

It's a great round of applause for making it this far! You are literally a hero in my eyes. You have defeated your insecurities, stood up to your fears, and overcome your negative traits. I am so proud of you! However, the journey is still ongoing. Get ready for the next chapter filled with self-healing activities that will motivate you to live your life to the fullest.

Change is Scary but Beautiful

You need to step out of your comfort zone and challenge yourself. I know that it might feel frightening to experience change. But once you do, you will feel like this is the most beautiful thing to experience. Change can give you new opportunities and help you live a better life.

This chapter is your first opportunity for a better life, so make the most of it. Let's move together toward the final step of our self-healing journey!

So let's get started!

Letting Go of Control

Letting go means learning from your past, accepting that there were very harmful times, and deciding to end your memories. Everybody wants to learn from bad experiences but struggles to overcome those hard times. It is essential to stop thinking about past traumas as they do you no good. All you have now is the present moment. So, learn to live in it and embrace every moment of it. When our old shoes become too small for us to wear, we must get new ones so that we may move freely and perform our jobs.

Similarly, to walk and function better in life, it's vital to modify old memories and experiences that do not fit or serve the current circumstance or life well. You can do this by adopting new ideas and beliefs. Though difficult, it's a must for happiness and productivity in life. Happiness stems from past experiences.

For people with narcissism, it might not be easy to let go of situations or people. This is because they have developed these insecurities of abandonment and not having enough control. As a result, they try to control everything in their life and even those of others. We might look more profound. This tight grip is holding us back from living our most significant moment from living times; holding onto a situation is more painful than letting go. Life does not go the way you want it to go, and thus, trying to gain control of every aspect may cause extreme levels of stress, anxiety, and fear. Letting go allows you to be mindful of and acknowledge the present situation fully. By letting go, you experience true inner peace and develop into a more patient and calming person.

Here is an activity that might help you to let go of things and practice inner peace.

- **Step 1:** Take a moment and reflect on when you feel you need to take control of the situation. What situations trigger your insecurities, and you become scared if things do not go your way? Write down all of these situations on a piece of paper.
- **Step 2:** After this, imagine letting go of control in these situations. Note down every feeling that you will experience in the moment. Write down all the fears regarding this situation.
- **Step 3:** Now, analyze whether these fears and doubts are based on reality or overwhelming emotions. Try to analyze your reactions and emotions if another person took control of a situation. For instance,

express your feelings if you have a business project and someone else takes the lead.

- **Step 4:** Now, try to suggest alternative ways of reacting based on logic and not your emotions and fears.

Practical Strategies for Change

Changing yourself for the better is the best gift you can give yourself. Although initially change may feel scary, it is beautiful in the end. Everyone has to go through life changes to evolve into something better. For instance, a seed has to go through various stages of growth to blossom into a flower. Similarly, a cocoon goes through phases of change to turn into a vibrant butterfly!

Do not be afraid of change; rather, believe that it will bring out something more positive!

Embracing change means accepting new opportunities, and you should give them a chance. It is time to get out of your comfort zone and challenge yourself.

Here are a few ways in which you can get out of your comfort zone.

1. Set Realistic Goals

The first step to becoming a better person is identifying the areas you lack. This could be your personality, your career, your relationships, or even your thoughts. You need to write down all the areas that need improvement and start working on them.

2. Write Down Your Manifestation

Imagine your best self and write about it in your journal. Try to provide as much detail as you can. The most important thing to this magic is to write down your manifestations. This is because the mind does not know the difference between reality and what you tell it. If you constantly think about your goals, your mind will automatically start to work towards them.

Once you have started practicing your goals, you should take small steps toward achieving them. Taking giant leaps forward, your goals will only leave you exhausted. If you are trying to achieve a big goal, breaking it down into smaller ones will help immensely. If you are trying to be friends with someone whom you do not like, you can set your goals as follows:

- **Self-Reflection:** Identify the things that you do not like in that person or the reason behind your disliking.
- **Shifting Your Perspective:** Try to understand that person by putting yourself in their shoes. Empathize with them and reflect on why they acted in such a way.
- **Initiate Small Interactions:** Say hello to them while they are walking past you.
- **Work Together on a Task:** Try to be friends with them and work with them. This will help you get to know each other better.
- **Deepen the Connection:** Offer help when needed and do not shy away from being open to them.

3. Shunning Polarized Thinking

Polarized thinking is a way of thinking in which a person only sees the other person at fault. They believe the other person wants to hurt and insult them and thus think of them as enemies. This is a black and white thinking that harms relationships. This is extremely common in narcissistic relationships.

Here is an activity designed to overcome polarized thinking and look at the other person's perspective.

- **Step 1:** The first step to overcoming polarized thinking is recognizing it. When you get a thought with extremities, detect it as polarized. For instance, "You are so terrible at tennis." However, there might be a possibility that the other person needs more practice.
- **Step 2:** Once you have recognized a polarized thought, place it on a scale of 1-10. Now, analyze the thought and view how extreme it is. If there are no counterarguments for this thought, then it can be a 10.

However, if you can make counterarguments, it moves down the scale until no counterarguments can be made.

- **Step 3:** Once you have learned to overcome polarized thinking, practice it daily. Whenever you have a polarized thought, start counter-arguing and try to see the facts rather than what your emotions tell you.

4. Embracing Spiritual Growth

Spirituality helps you identify the deeper parts of your inner self and connects you with your life's true purpose. Embracing spirituality to look for the real meaning of life disconnects you from the materialistic aspects of the world. It helps you to focus entirely on yourself and get to know yourself like no other way. Having a spiritual heart can allow you to feel and understand things more deeply. Your heart fills with love and positivity, and you feel like giving it to the whole world.

- *Here is an activity that will help you gain a better understanding of your spiritual journey.*
- **Step 1:** Find a place that comforts you the most. Now, sit in this place with no disturbance. Close your eyes and start reflecting on the core values that you have developed since you were a child.
- **Step 2:** Write down the things that bring you true happiness and the ones you are truly passionate about. Analyze how these things align with your life and can improve you.
- **Step 3:** Once you have identified the acts that you truly love, start listing ways in which you can carry them out. Decide the time and place for carrying out this activity and write it down, so you can remember it.
- **Step 4:** Create a reflection journal for these activities and express how you feel when you carry them out. Try to note down every detail, so that you can reflect on them at the end of each month.

5. Managing Relapses

Walking on the path of healing is never easy, and there are many hardships that one has to face.

However, with a dedicated heart, you will surely reach your goals and destination. The most important thing you need to remember is that growth is never linear. There are many times when you want to give up or experience a relapse. But true strength lies in getting up again, brushing the dust off, and starting the journey again. Sometimes, you feel exhausted and want to take a break. In these situations, take it easy on yourself and take small steps toward your goal.

Here is a recovery toolbox specially designed to help you during a relapse.

Take a large sheet of paper and draw a toolbox with various compartments. Label each compartment with different strategies and tricks. Now, start to fill each compartment with tools that might help you out in times of relapse. It also includes activities that you want to try or look forward to.

Here are some examples that you can use for your compartments.

- **Self-Care Tools:** This compartment will contain all the things that help you calm down or make you feel relaxed. These could be fidgeting toys or your favorite stuffed animals.
- **Self-Care Herbs:** This compartment will comprise herbs that can help you reduce anxiety or panic attacks. Examples of these herbs include chamomile, valerian, and lavender.
- **My Emergency Contacts:** This compartment will comprise the contact of those people who love and care for you. You can contact these people whenever you have a rough day or want emotional support.

Living Your Best Life

As you near the end of this self-healing journey, you open the door to a life filled with renewed hope and emotional freedom. With each step forward, you'll nurture kindness and empathy, embracing a positive outlook that guides you toward becoming the best version of yourself.

Refraining from Negativity

It is important to take control of your thoughts and live a positive life. If a person experiences negative thoughts constantly, then there are more chances of being depressed and acting in narcissistic ways. You should learn to deal with negative things and not let them stress you out much.

Here is a fun activity to help you overcome your negative thoughts.

- **Step 1:** Take a jar and decorate it as your choice. Add stickers, labels, or anything else you want! After this, place the jar in a safe spot out of children's reach.
- **Step 2:** Whenever a negative thought pops up, pause everything momentarily. Start to reflect on why you experienced that thought and focus on it for a minute. After this, let go of that thought and think of a positive thing you encountered as an alternative.
- **Step 3:** Write down the positive experience on a small paper. Please fold the paper and put it inside the jar that you decorated.
- **Step 4:** At the end of the week, reflect on the positivity in your life by opening up the chits in the jar and reading them aloud!

Acting with Kindness

Kindness is a beautiful act that makes those around you happy and brings you peace. The warmth of kindness is just like a ripple effect that spreads everywhere and increases in size. Treating everyone with kindness fosters deeper relations with the people. You can find your life's true purpose by integrating small acts of kindness into your daily life.

Kindness is the act of helping another person without gaining any benefit from them. It can be as simple as making a cup of tea for someone or as big as lending them vast amounts of money.

Here are a few ways to practice kindness in your daily life.

- **Step 1:** Take a few blank chits and write an act of kindness on each one. Place these chits inside a jar that is visible to you.
- **Step 2:** Take out one chit when you get up in the morning. Whatever is written on that chit is the goal that you have to accomplish that day.
- **Step 3:** Find ways to accomplish your goals of kindness and do them with complete love and care.

Learning from Every Lesson

Learning is usually considered to be done only in an institution and refers to gaining subject knowledge. However, we fail to realize that as long as our hearts beat, we can learn from everything in our lives. Human beings are created to gain knowledge, and their education is not confined to subjects. We all make mistakes, and instead of dwelling on them, we must learn from them. Every lesson we encounter is placed in our lives to teach us something. It was never put to hurt or break you; it was meant to turn you into a better person.

The journey of learning continues with us until our last breath, so why don't we shake hands and accept each other?

Here are a few ways in which you can turn every mistake and bad experience into a lesson.

Make a learning journal for yourself. Whenever you make a mistake or encounter a bad experience, write it down in that journal. Besides the experience, please write down the lessons you learned and how they shaped you into a better person. Also, express your feelings and reactions related to that experience. After a month, open your journal and review the lessons that you have learned over time.

Actionable Advice

Following a set of rules and regulations is essential to achieve something. The most crucial thing in achieving your goals is discipline and consistency. To become a better version of yourself, you must be disciplined and motivate yourself to do better every time. The growth plan is designed for you to achieve your goals realistically. It will move you forward on the path of self-healing and allow you to live a peaceful life. This plan focuses on fostering relationships, building healthy self-esteem, and cultivating a positive mindset. By following this plan, you will soon break free from the selfish roots holding you back. You will live a life of balance, love, and peace.

At G.R.O.W.T.H., the road to a more fulfilling and peaceful existence begins.

1. Grateful Mindset:

List three things you are thankful for at the beginning of each day. This helps you stop thinking about yourself and focus on the good things in your life and the lives of people around you.

2. Realistic Goals:

Divide your more ambitious goals into smaller portions. Put more emphasis on your growth and contentment than on approval from others.

3. Open Communication:

Engage in conversations by actively listening. Try to empathize with others' emotions instead of drawing attention to yourself.

4. Welcome Growth:

Get a genuine opinion from someone you can trust, then consider it without getting defensive. Please make use of it to pinpoint your areas of growth and improvement.

5. Trust-Building:

Honor your word and demonstrate empathy by considering the effects of your actions on other people. Strive to mend relationships by showing understanding and consistency.

6. Humility Practice:

Recognize when you need assistance or need all the answers. Make it a habit to acknowledge the contributions of others and be open to what you can learn from everyone. Be humble and adopt the habit of giving credit to others for their contributions to your achievements.

Give yourself the biggest applaud because you have come to the end of this book! I am so proud of you and look forward to seeing you develop into much more!

Bonus Section: Your Survival Kit for Handling Narcissists with Ease

10 Strategies for Handling a Narcissistic Partner

Being in a relationship with a narcissist can be challenging and even make you feel overwhelmed from time to time. However, if you equip yourself with the right tools, you can navigate your relationship quickly. This will not only prove to be beneficial for your relationship but will also keep your mental and emotional well-being protected.

This chapter is designed for people who are trying to make their relationship work and are not giving up! It provides ten practical strategies for handling your partner who has a narcissistic personality disorder. These strategies are easy to apply and would save you much effort and time. This chapter covers it all, whether you are learning, setting boundaries, or even managing your expectations!

Now, practice these strategies and start dealing with your narcissistic partner.

1. Learn about Narcissistic Personality Disorder

You should clearly understand and familiarize yourself with the subject to deal with something. You need to be aware of the signs of the narcissist's personality so that it would be easier for you to identify them.

It is also crucial that you learn about their trauma or the experiences that caused them to become a narcissist. In this way, you can avoid triggering their insecurities and thus handle your relationship smoothly.

Here are simple ways to gain knowledge regarding narcissism.

• Try to attend workshops and read books or articles based on narcissistic personality disorder. This helps you to explore the area and gain a better understanding of the disorder.

• Try to connect with people who have had a similar experience to you. These people could be those handling a narcissistic partner, friend, or even a family member.

• You can also seek consultation from a therapist specializing in this field.

2. Set Clear Boundaries

Narcissists find it hard to respect other people's boundaries and often cross the line. This hurts the other person and makes them question their worth. There would have been many times when your partner did the same thing. Thus, it is essential to set clear boundaries with a narcissistic partner and ensure that they cannot cross those boundaries. Setting boundaries with a narcissist is the most critical step to control them.

Here are a few steps to help you define clear boundaries that your partner should not cross at all costs.

• Think of the areas where you want to put the boundaries and to what extent. Make sure to explain to your partner in detail about your boundaries.

• Use an assertive tone that shows that you are firm in your boundaries, but do not try to disrespect your partner or target them.

• Ensure that your partner listens carefully to you and starts respecting your boundaries. If they do something that disrespects your boundaries, confront them but in a lighter tone.

3. Communicate in a Wise Manner

If you want to live a peaceful life with your partner, try to use clear and short statements with them. This will not create any misunderstanding in their mind.

Here are a few ways in which you can talk wisely with your partner

- Keep your responses short and to the point. Also, use a firm tone without any emotions so that it clearly indicates to the narcissist that manipulating is pointless.

- If a narcissist tries to start an argument with you, show no emotions and speak with logic. In this way, you can avoid the argument and the conflict.

- Try to maintain your focus on the topic that you are discussing. Avoid getting triggered or distracted by their emotional responses or their negative words.

4. Do Not Take Things Personally

You should not take things personally if a narcissist does something against you. This is because they have their own insecurities that they try to hide. Blaming you for something they have done is just an act of protecting their insecurities.

Narcissists play such tactics that you start to believe that you are the culprit and they are the victim. You start to question yourself and dismiss your logic and emotions. This can have a very harmful impact on your mental well-being and cripple your life.

5. Don't Give Response to Everything

Sometimes, you need to let go of issues and stop making a fuss. There are many times when you should let go of small conflicts and compromise when you are in a relationship with a narcissist. You need to realize that narcissists are fighting their own battles alone, and thus, you need to show empathy towards them. Understanding their situation will help you to maintain a healthy relationship with them.

Here are a few ways in which you can ignore small issues and let go of them easily.

• You need to differentiate between issues that are important to you and those that just bring out a negative impact on all.

• If the issue is not that important, you can let it go and not discuss it.

• However, if the issue continues to provoke you or hurt you, try communicating it with your partner in a calming way. Do not trigger them by blaming them or making them at fault. Try communicating, so that you both find solutions to the problem.

6. Practice Self Care

It is essential to take care of yourself when you are going through a tough time. Self-care gives you strength and makes you feel confident about yourself. Indulging in regular self-care exercises can boost your mood and mental well-being. Being in a relationship with a narcissist can cause a lot of fatigue and distress. Self-care activities, like meditation, hot baths, etc., can relieve your stress and bring out positivity in you.

Here are simple ways in which you can practice self-care and take control of your emotions.

• Schedule a "Me Time" for yourself at the end of the day. During this time, do activities that will help you recharge. These include reading, writing, dancing, or even talking to a friend.

• Every morning, try to meditate for at least 10-15 minutes a day. Practice deep breathing, gratitude, and mindful observation in your morning rituals.

• Try to maintain your relationships by meeting your loved ones at least once a week. They will provide emotional support and love to motivate you to look forward to life.

7. Have No Expectations

Being in a relationship with a narcissistic person means that your emotional needs are often neglected. This is because narcissists are suffering from their own emotions and thus fail to understand yours. They also lack empathy and are always the center of attention. This way, your emotions and feelings might get neglected, and you soon start feeling overwhelmed. The most important thing to do in such a situation is to cut off any expectations from your partner. If you constantly expect your partner to comfort you and they fail to do so, you will get extremely hurt. You need to realize that you are your hero and must save yourself.

Here are a few ways to manage your expectations and take control of your feelings.

- Try to take control of your expectations by understanding that your partner is going through a mental disorder. You need to have no expectations from them and thus do not force them to do things.
- You should start doing things that make you happy. It could be a dancing, singing or even a cooking class

8. Keep Control of Yourself

It is important to be considerate about your feelings when you are dealing with a narcissistic partner. You should prioritize your happiness and protection.

Here are a few ways to protect your mental and emotional well-being.

- Try to do things that make you the happiest. These can be all the activities that you love doing like painting, cooking or even riding a bicycle.
- Identify your core values and morals and stick to them. Never let go of these values, even if they differ from your partner's.
- Surround yourself with people who give you genuine advice and motivate you to improve.

9. Be Respectful

When you are in a relationship with a narcissist, you need to respect their traumas and their abusive experiences. You need to remember that most of their toxic actions are just behaviors that they have developed due to hurtful experiences in the past. There is no right to hurt or abuse them in return as they are diagnosed with a mental disorder. They are unlike familiar people and must be treated with care and concern.

You need to stop disrespecting the narcissists in return and understand their insecurities and where they are coming from. It would help if you were patient while dealing with such people, as they have fragile and broken souls.

Here are a few ways to show them respect and deal with them effectively.

- Provide them with emotional support when they seem upset or triggered.
- When they are emotional, try to understand their perspectives and look at the situation through their eyes.
- Do not try to put on unnecessary fights and drama, as they already deal with enough.

10. Planning Your Exit

For a relationship to work, both partners should put in effort. However, rarely, a narcissistic partner would also start to put in effort with real feelings. Thus, most of the narcissist relationships fail. There is a possibility that your relationship could also fail despite giving your best. You need to realize that you need to leave a relationship before it gets abusive or too controlling. This will destroy your mental peace and your life.

Here are a few ways in which you can plan your exit.

- Start looking for a new apartment or house where you can live on your own. Make sure to sort out how you'll pay for it and handle any other financial needs.
- If you're married or have kids, you might need to deal with legal matters. This means you might need to talk to a lawyer to understand what you need to do about custody, property, or other shared things.

- Let your friends and family know what's happening. They can offer support and help you through this tough time.

It might be challenging to leave a toxic partner, but your emotional and physical well-being should come as the top priority for you!

10 Ways to Deal with a Narcissist in Your Home

Dealing with a narcissistic parent or a sibling can affect your emotional and mental well-being a lot. Unlike other relationships, the bond with family members is different. You share a bloodline and have an emotional attachment to them. Their words and actions matter the most to you and have the most significant influence. It can be challenging to deal with the harsh words or toxic actions that they do, and it destroys your self-esteem and self-worth. However, you continue to be patient and deal with them because you love them.

A narcissistic parent creates such a home environment that children feel inadequate and suffer from low self-esteem. They show no interest in their children, belittle them, and even give love based on conditions. Such an environment harms the children and develops insecurities in them.

Here are a few ways in which you can deal with a narcissistic family member without compromising on your mental and emotional well-being.

1. Create Emotional Distance

Children are emotionally attached to their parents or family members, and thus, it is hard for them to detach. However, it is essential that you emotionally detach yourself from the family member who is causing you constant harm. Just as the support and love from family matter the most, so do the harsh words and actions. Children are most influenced by how their family members react to them. Thus, it is necessary to maintain your distance from the narcissistic members and protect your well-being.

Here are a few ways to create emotional distance from your parents without causing them too much pain.

• It would help if you accept that your family member is toxic and has hurt you numerous times.

• You must admit that they don't tend to show love.

• It is okay if your feelings get overwhelmed and you experience extreme sadness or grief. Feel them thoroughly, and then let yourself free!

If it is impossible to maintain the physical distance, try to create the emotional distance. Start to mentally detach yourself from them and stop getting affected by their words or actions. Feel as if there is an emotional barrier between you and them. This barrier protects you from all the negativity that they throw at you.

Wisely prepare yourself for severe backlash and manipulation by that parent or family member.

2. Change Your Expectations

You need to accept that your parents are different from other parents. Thus, it would help if you stop building expectations from them and hope they will change. You need to realize that you have to protect yourself on your own and be your caretaker. Letting go of all the expectations allows you to protect yourself from resentment and disappointments. See the reality and start accepting it for your good. Accepting that your parent has a disorder helps you to reduce stress and anxiety. You begin viewing them as a patient instead of a parent. The negativity they throw on you is all just insecurities hidden inside themselves.

Here is an activity that will help you to let go of expectations and stop being disappointed.

• **Step 1:** Take a piece of paper and write down the expectations you have from your parents.

• **Step 2:** After this, write down their actions and behaviors in daily life.

- **Step 3:** Now, reflect on whether their reactions align with your expectations. Deeply analyze their actions and start to accept reality.

- **Step 4:** Make a list of things that you expect to have in your life. These can include love, care, respect, etc. Now, start giving all those things to yourself.

3. Talk with Yourself

Your parents might throw tantrums or even blame you for what you did not do, leaving you questioning yourself and your worth. Overcoming challenges to overcome your intense emotions when your parents disrespect you might be difficult. However, it is important to know your true self and give it all the love and respect that it deserves.

It would help if you firmly believe in yourself and your actions. You need to accept that your parents are only blaming you because they do not want to take the blame.

Here is an activity to know you honestly and stay committed.

Step 1: Sit down in a quiet place when you have conflicts with your parents, and they insult you.

Step 2: Now, try to feel their words profoundly and let all of your emotions out.

Step 3: Once you have let your emotions out, think logically. Are their words valid or just a projection of their insecurities?

4. Start Planning to Be Independent

Think of moving away from your narcissistic parents when you feel that they are being abusive or too controlling. This is because no one should compromise on their mental and emotional health.

Here are a few techniques to help you out with this.

- **Set Goals:** Determine what you need to achieve before leaving (e.g., stable income, savings, a place to live).

- **Budget:** Plan your finances carefully. Start saving money to cover rent, utilities, and other essentials.

- **Find Support:** Identify friends, family, or professionals who can support you during this transition.

5. Empower Yourself with Knowledge

Knowledge not only brings wisdom but also helps one to be well aware of what's happening around them. This is one of the most critical factors to inner peace. Be well aware. By being well aware of narcissism, you will be better able to identify the traits in your parents and deal with them.

Growth and knowledge are directly proportional to each other. If the knowledge is of your academic field, it helps you move forward in life. If knowledge is spiritual, it enables you to grow a deeper connection with your creator. If you want to grow, learn. There's an old saying that goes by collecting knowledge from wherever you can and letting you analyze, choose, and decide what is right and wrong.

There may have been many times when your parents started abusing you or making you feel worthless. You may have started questioning your worth and gone into depression. You may have felt like you are useless and have no purpose in life. But let me ask you a question. What would happen if a household bulb is given an electric washing machine supply? No wonder it will burn and fuse.

Realizing your worth and knowing your passion is essential. If anybody abuses you, you will no longer question your worth.

It is crucial to let yourself grow with time. For a kick start, learn about something you like, whether it is cooking, a video game, photography, or anything else. All this time, you have been just doing your thing with interest. This time, incorporate knowledge into it, too, and see the results and improvement you get. After practicing this, move to more interesting and challenging topics. Knowledge opens the mind and gives an enlarged view of all the scenarios one faces in life.

Here is an activity for you to know about yourself deeper.

- **Choose a Subject:** Choose any one subject of your interest. It can be something in general that interests you or something you would like to know about, a hobby, or something scientific or historical. There isn't even a need to stick within your field.
- **Keep a Timer:** Spend 30 minutes on this exercise.
- **Research and Gather Information:** In the specified time, dig deeper into your chosen topic. You may refer to the internet, some books, or even interview people. Note down a minimum of 5 interesting facts, pieces of information, or new insights.
- **Reflect:** When your timer goes off, reflect on what you have just learned for a couple of minutes. Write down how this knowledge could pertain to your life or how it changes your perspective.

Share what you learned with friends and family members or on social media. Telling someone about it helps crystallize the learning and might spark an excellent discussion.

6. Set Boundaries Around Criticism

Have you ever wondered or given a thought to what ignites a spark in you? Yes, you are right.

Sometimes, it's our self-motivation, but we can be motivated or demotivated due to being cozy in our comfort zone. For instance, you get ready for school or dinner. The thing is that we need to prepare and know what we are looking like. What is wrong with our outfit? What needs correction? How are we going to know all of that stuff? It is the mirror that helps us see. If the mirror is not there, it is almost impossible to correct our look, etc.

Similarly, to know where we are headed in life, what steps do we need to take? Are the steps we consider taking healthy for us? To know all that, we need a life mirror, which is nothing else but other people around us. They see us and our steps, sometimes more clearly than ourselves. This is why criticism is essential, and dealing with criticism positively is even more critical. Take criticism as a growth cheat code.

Your parents might criticize you due to their narcissistic traits and insecurities. You need to realize that they are doing this because they are dealing with subpar stuff and thus want others to feel the same as well.

I know their words can be wrong, but use their criticism as a cheat code for growth.

Human nature is that we are the best at what we do, but criticism might hurt us. That bit ignites the real spark for being better and best at our job. While letting the criticism work for us, know the difference between real criticism and jealousy-based criticism. A way to differentiate between the both is to take the criticism and sit down with your thoughts. Ask yourself, "Is that the case?" and you will never lie to yourself. Don't hear what you want to, but hear the authentic voice inside you. It is always there. If confusion still occurs, ask a loved one for an opinion and then decide.

Activity:

List It Out: Think of three recent pieces of criticism you've received. Write them down on a piece of paper or in a journal.

Analyze the Source: Next to each criticism, write down who gave it to you and their relationship to you (e.g., friend, colleague, family member). Consider if they are someone who generally has your best interests at heart.

Filter the Feedback:

• For each criticism, ask yourself: "Is this feedback meant to help me grow, or is it coming from a place of negativity?"

• Circle the constructive criticisms that can help you improve. Draw a line through the ones that seem negative or unhelpful.

Take Action: For the constructive criticisms, write one action you can take to address them. Write a positive affirmation about yourself for the negative criticisms to counteract any lingering doubt.

Bonus Tip: Practice this activity regularly to build a strong "criticism filter" that helps you set healthy boundaries while growing from helpful feedback.

7. Focus on Self-Validation

I heard you put a lot of hard work into your work. I heard that you took your job very seriously. I heard that you wore those clothes with much excitement. I heard that you practiced that sport too hard. When you are the one working on yourself solely, then it is a must. It would help if you were the sole judge of your progress and not the people. Prioritize yourself. If you put in all that effort and are satisfied with what you did, then there is no need to let others demotivate or dishearten you regarding your work. Our minds get attached to cheap and easily accessible dopamine fast. One example is cheesy words by others and no likes after posting something on social media apps. All this has changed our minds, even our own. Come out of this bubble. Be happy about your progress even if there are zero likes, even if there are zero cheesy words around you. Your own words should be enough for you.

The experiences you go through are solely yours. The struggle is yours. Be happy with it. No one can feel what you feel doing all these things. So wait for no one to tell you that you are good.

Appreciate yourself enough that you don't need it from others. After all, many people get jealous, and very few get happy with what we do. Your primary focus should be quality dopamine, which comes from hard work and sweat. That satisfaction will grant you inner peace and take you to new heights. Believe in your ability to make decisions and understand your own needs.

Here is an activity that will help you in developing self-confidence.

- **Step 1:** Go to your nearest park and walk on the track.

- **Step 2:** Start observing your environment as you walk. Notice the plants, leaves, birds and everything present in the park.
- **Step 3:** Now, start talking positively about yourself and think of all the good deeds you have done.
- **Step 4:** Reflect on these deeds and embrace every moment of this activity.

8. Limit Their Influence on Your Life Decisions

You need to realize that it is your life, and the decisions are yours. Your parents might try to interfere in your life, and thus, you need to limit their influence. You need to ensure that you deserve to live a unique and successful life. You have to work on yourself and your dreams and you deserve your own space and identity.

The first step to success? Take that step first. Once the step is taken, it will someday lead to success. Nobody understands you better than you. You are a whole human being with decision power and a sight to see. If you think that little step will be a successful asset one day, take the step. Small steps are always a better approach. Take each step as you climb on a ladder.

Let's consider what happens if the plan doesn't work well. Will you fail? Be grateful for failure.

Everything in life teaches you a lesson. It prepares you for something big. You need to trust your energies and start trusting your healing process.

Here is an activity that will help you deal with your parents.

Step 1: Make a good decision that you have been afraid to make all your life.

Step 2: Break it down in the following way:

- Write the decision at the top of the page.
- Below, list small, actionable steps taken toward moving forward.
- Arrange these steps as steps on a ladder toward the goal.

Step 3: Promise yourself to stick to your decision and take the right steps for it.

Step 4: Now, start making the right choices for that decision. Write down each and every detail regarding your decision in your journal and reflect on whether you made the right choice or not.

Review and Revise: Once you have climbed to the top step of your ladder, review the process from start to finish. Did you reach your goal? What have you learned? If things don't turn out as expected, refine your approach and build another ladder from experience.

9. Prepare for Backlash When Setting Boundaries

You must know how to set boundaries for people. Selfish people are takers; you must decide how much of your peace you will let them take.

It would help if you prioritize yourself. Your inner peace must be protected at all costs. For that purpose, you need to set boundaries correctly. Stop them right at the moment if the way they are joking is out of limits. Tell them right away if their actions are not right in your view. Do not be a people pleaser. Be kind enough, but know the difference. If you don't stop someone from doing what you feel is wrong each time, you practically let them treat you the same way or even worse the next time. So, tell people what you think because inner peace is crucial for growth in any sector of life. Your mind must be calm and stress-free.

If you take this step for yourself and stop people from setting the boundaries right away, you will see a massive change. They will try to manipulate you into thinking that you are wrong. Be aware of the right and wrong. As humans, we want to have control over others.

We want to be dominant, and this trait can hurt one's ego too fast if they see you taking control of your life and decisions. You must be prepared to face all that and deal with it tactically. Still, be mindful, kind, and aware enough to be the sailor of your ship.

Activity:

1. Think of a Situation: Picture a time when you needed to set a boundary but didn't, or think of something that might happen in the future. Maybe it's at work where someone keeps interrupting you or a friend who teases you in a way that doesn't feel right.

2. Plan What You'll Say: Write down what you would say to set the boundary. Keep it clear and polite, like, "I'd like to finish what I'm saying before we move on," or "I know you're joking, but those comments don't sit well with me. Can you stop?"

3. Imagine Their Reaction: Think about how the person might react. Could they say you're overreacting? Might they get defensive? Write down their expected reactions.

4. Prepare Your Comeback: Describe how you'd respond calmly to each possible reaction. For instance, your parents might say that you are overreacting. Now, write down your response in as many details as possible. Start practicing this response. Once you are done practicing, take a moment to reflect on how you feel about everything.

Real-life Motivational Story

From Narcissism to Love

Hannah and Shawn were high school sweethearts and loved each other. Hannah adored Shawn's charismatic personality and his handsome face. Shawn had always been the center of attention, and everyone liked him.

Shawn and Hannah were living happily in their fairytale world. However, as time passed, Hannah noticed slight changes in Shawn's behavior. He would get upset over little things and express rage. When Hannah confronted him about his behaviors, he became defensive and put all the blame on her. Hannah soon realized that his boyfriend had narcissistic personality disorder.

However, she did not give up on her relationship. She started to do things that would make Shawn happy. She would not make a big deal out of everything and would express her feelings respectfully. No matter what Hannah did, it went to waste. Shawn would express the same anger and ego issues.

One day, after a considerable fight, Hannah decided that she could no longer live like this. She warned Shawn to go to therapy or else she would end things with him. At first, Shawn did not agree, but eventually, Hannah convinced him.

They both went to therapy to become a better couple. During his therapy sessions, Shawn discovered many deep-rooted insecurities and fears that had built up inside him throughout his life. He started healing those insecurities to break free from the chains of narcissism. Hannah also went to therapy to regain her self-confidence and self-esteem.

Soon, Shawn started to change his behaviors. He would no longer get defensive or express dominance over everyone. He would communicate with Hannah healthily and positively. Their relationship flourished, and they lived happily ever after!

The purpose of the story is to let you know that, if your narcissism is severe, I mean if it is NPD, then you should consider visiting a therapist.

Conclusion

This book has been more than just a guide; it has been a steadfast companion on your journey toward a better life. As you reach the final page, take a moment to reflect on the progress you've made. You chose to confront your inner struggles and face your fears with courage. In doing so, you've shown remarkable strength.

This journey has been about bringing the shadowed parts of your personality into the light. You've learned toxic cycles and are now stepping into the world with renewed self-esteem and confidence. You've delved deep into your insecurities and, despite moments of doubt, persevered in your efforts to grow. I hope that your relationships will start to flourish and that you'll become someone others trust and confide in. Even in conflict, you will approach situations with empathy, logic, and understanding.

You've untangled the grip of narcissism and now it's time for living with a sense of freedom. Remember, this book isn't an ending but a beginning. You are now equipped with the tools and knowledge to continue your journey of transformation. Each day offers a new opportunity to challenge yourself and grow into the person you aspire to be.

The light within you shines brighter than ever. Carry it with you as you move forward, knowing that the best is yet to come.

References

1. Achieve Centre. (n.d.). *6 steps to constructive conflict resolution.* Retrieved from https://achievecentre.com/blog/6-steps-constructive-conflict-resolution/
2. Atlasian. (n.d.). *Active listening.* Retrieved from https://www.atlassian.com/blog/communication/active-listening?utm_source=gdn&utm_medium=paid-display&campaign=21252494340&adgroup=&device=c&devicemodel=&placement=&aceid=&creative=&adtype=&gclid=EAIaIQobChMI_Ifmm9HmhwMVtpODBx2CcS4LEAAYASAAEgJyGvD_BwE&country=&network=x&targetid=&gad_source=1
3. Charlie Health. (n.d.). *The long-term effects of narcissistic abuse.* Retrieved from https://www.charliehealth.com/post/the-long-term-effects-of-narcissistic-abuse
4. Cleveland Clinic. (n.d.). *Narcissistic personality disorder.* Retrieved from https://my.clevelandclinic.org/health/diseases/9742-narcissistic-personality-disorder
5. Corporate Finance Institute. (n.d.). *Communication.* Retrieved from https://corporatefinanceinstitute.com/resources/management/communication/
6. Health Direct. (n.d.). *Building and maintaining healthy relationships.* Retrieved from https://www.healthdirect.gov.au/building-and-maintaining-healthy-relationships
7. Healthline. (n.d.). *How to deal with a narcissist.* Retrieved from https://www.healthline.com/health/how-to-deal-with-a-narcissist

8. HelpGuide.org. (n.d.). *Narcissistic personality disorder*. Retrieved from https://www.helpguide.org/articles/mental-disorders/narcissistic-personality-disorder.htm
9. McLean Hospital. (n.d.). *NPD provider guide*. Retrieved from https://www.mcleanhospital.org/npd-provider-guide
10. Mental Health Foundation. (n.d.). *Top tips for building and maintaining healthy relationships*. Retrieved from https://www.mentalhealth.org.uk/our-work/public-engagement/healthy-relationships/top-tips-building-and-maintaining-healthy-relationships
11. Medium. (2023). *Ripple effects of narcissistic behavior on adults and their children*. Retrieved from https://medium.com/illumination/ripple-effects-of-narcissistic-behavior-on-adults-and-their-children-b41e857e53e3
12. Medium. (2023). *Sit in your own mess: Embrace the silence*. Retrieved from https://medium.com/@ameenelelu/sit-in-your-own-mess-embrace-the-silence-f4360bbe0993
13. Mayo Clinic. (n.d.). *Narcissistic personality disorder: Symptoms and causes*. Retrieved from https://www.mayoclinic.org/diseases-conditions/narcissistic-personality-disorder/symptoms-causes/syc-20366662
14. Mind. (n.d.). *Tips to improve your self-esteem*. Retrieved from https://www.mind.org.uk/information-support/types-of-mental-health-problems/self-esteem/tips-to-improve-your-self-esteem/
15. Narcissistic Abuse Rehab. (n.d.). *The long-term consequences of narcissistic abuse*. Retrieved from https://www.narcissisticabuserehab.com/the-long-term-consequences-of-narcissistic-abuse/
16. Open Psychometrics. (n.d.). *NPI test*. Retrieved from https://openpsychometrics.org/tests/NPI/1.php
17. Parent and Teen. (n.d.). *Positive peer pressure*. Retrieved from https://parentandteen.com/positive-peer-pressure/
18. Psychology Today. (2023). *How narcissism rates differ depending on age and sex*. Retrieved from

https://www.psychologytoday.com/intl/blog/close-encounters/202306/how-narcissism-rates-differ-depending-on-age-and-sex#:~:text=Gender%20Differences%20in%20Narcissism,-Narcissism%20involves%20agency&text=Men%2C%20on%20average%2C%20tend%20to,levels%20of%20narcissism%20than%20women

19. Psych DB. (n.d.). *Narcissistic personality disorder.* Retrieved from https://www.psychdb.com/personality/narcissistic
20. Psych Central. (n.d.). *How to deal with a narcissistic partner.* Retrieved from https://psychcentral.com/blog/how-deal-narcissistic-partner
21. Taylor Counseling Group. (n.d.). *Narcissistic manipulation.* Retrieved from https://taylorcounselinggroup.com/blog/narcissistic-manipulation/#:~:text=Narcissists%20will%20make%20all%20the,regain%20control%20over%20the%20victim
22. Thoughtful Threads. (n.d.). *The ripples of sacrifice: How narcissistic behavior affects health and wellbeing.* Retrieved from https://www.thoughtfulthreads.ai/post/the-ripples-of-sacrifice-how-narcissistic-behavior-affects-health-and-wellbeing
23. Thriveworks. (n.d.). *What is narcissism?* Retrieved from https://thriveworks.com/help-with/narcissism/what-is-narcissism/
24. Verywell Mind. (n.d.). *What is empathy?* Retrieved from https://www.verywellmind.com/what-is-empathy-2795562
25. Verywell Mind. (n.d.). *Why it's important to have high self-esteem.* Retrieved from https://www.verywellmind.com/why-it-s-important-to-have-high-self-esteem-5094127
26. WebMD. (n.d.). *Narcissistic personality disorder.* Retrieved from https://www.webmd.com/mental-health/narcissistic-personality-disorder
27. WHO. (n.d.). *Mental disorders.* Retrieved from https://www.who.int/news-room/fact-sheets/detail/mental-

disorders/?gad_source=1&gclid=EAIaIQobChMI-K7g2LHlhwMVrzwGAB3A5RfIEAAYASAAEgJ8T_D_BwE

28. LinkedIn. (n.d.). *What really is narcissism? The myth of the over-valued child.* Retrieved from https://www.linkedin.com/pulse/what-really-narcissism-myth-over-valued-child-brad-reedy
29. Everyday Feminism. (2016). *Narcissistic personality myths.* Retrieved from https://everydayfeminism.com/2016/05/narcissistic-personality-myths/
30. Medium. (2023). *Debunking the myth of narcissism.* Retrieved from https://medium.com/@jh_simon/debunking-the-myth-of-narcissism-b5aeeb7d3aea
31. Verywell Mind. (n.d.). *How to deal with a narcissistic parent.* Retrieved from https://www.verywellmind.com/how-to-deal-with-a-narcissistic-parent-7373070

Printed in Dunstable, United Kingdom

71481146R00070